JEWISH
CHOICES,
JEWISH
VOICES

SOCIAL
JUSTICE

This book has been made possible by the

generosity of the

Everett Foundation

JEWISH
CHOICES,
JEWISH
VOICES

SOCIAL
JUSTICE

EDITED BY
ELLIOT N. DORFF
AND
DANYA RUTTENBERG

2010 • 5770
The Jewish Publication Society
Philadelphia

Copyright © 2010 by Elliot N. Dorff and Danya Ruttenberg
First edition. All rights reserved.

No part of this book may be reproduced or transmitted in any form or by any means, electronic or mechanical, including photocopy, recording, or any information storage or retrieval system, except for brief passages in connection with a critical review, without permission in writing from the publisher:

The Jewish Publication Society
2100 Arch Street, 2nd floor
Philadelphia, PA 19103
www.jewishpub.org

Design and Composition by Progressive Information Technologies
Manufactured in the United States of America

09 10 11 12   10 9 8 7 6 5 4 3 2 1
ISBN: 978–0–8276–0860–3   (v.1. BODY)
ISBN: 978–0–8276–0861–0   (v.2. MONEY)
ISBN: 978–0–8276–0862–7   (v.3. POWER)
ISBN: 978–0–8276–0905–1   (v.4. SEX AND INTIMACY)
ISBN: 978–0–8276–0906–8   (v.5. WAR AND NATIONAL SECURITY)
ISBN: 978–0–8276–0907–5   (v.6. SOCIAL JUSTICE)

Library of Congress Cataloging-in-Publication Data:
Jewish choices, Jewish voices / edited by Elliot N. Dorff, Louis E. Newman. — 1st ed.
    v. cm.
    Includes bibliographical references and index.
    Contents: v. 1. Body
    ISBN 978-0-8276-0860-3 (ALK. PAPER)
    1. Jewish ethics.   2. Jews—Identity.   3. Body, Human—Religious aspects—Judaism.   I. Dorff, Elliot N.   II. Newman, Louis E.

    BJ1285.2.J49 2008
    296.3'6—dc22   2007037402

CONTENTS

Acknowledgments

No book—let alone a series of books—comes about without the creative energy and support of many people. We wish to thank, first and foremost, Ellen Frankel, Editor Emerita of The Jewish Publication Society, for her vision in first conceiving of this series and for her willingness to entrust it to our editorship. The JPS National Council played a critical role early on as the scope and format of the series were in the development stage. Julia Oestreich was invaluable and indefatigable as the Project Manager of this volume, acting with care, thoroughness and thoughtfulness at every turn, helping us to keep track of what needed to be done, making wonderful suggestions about possible contributors, and providing us with astute and constructive comments about earlier drafts of every part of this volume, including our own writing. Along with Julia Oestreich and the editors, Rabbis Uzi Weingarten and Steven Edelman-Blank collected, respectively, the classical and the contemporary Jewish sources for this volume. We are indebted to them for their fine work in locating these materials. We also wish to thank Monica Barr, Assistant Project Manager, who helped us immensely in contacting our contributors, making sure that they received and signed the proper contracts, and working with them to ensure that their contributions came in on time and that we had the latest versions of their essays in hand. We would additionally like to thank Julia Oestreich and Janet Liss for their skillful copyediting work, including organizing and coordinating scores of details necessary to ready this volume for publication. Their diligence and attention to detail are evident on every page of this book. Finally, we especially want to thank our contributors, whose creativity and thoughtfulness make this anthology the stimulating and deeply Jewish book that it is.

E.N.D.
D.R.

Introduction

"Whoever has the power to protest against members of his household but does not protest is punished for the transgressions of the members of his household. Against the people of his town, but does not, is punished for the deeds of those in his town. Against the entire world and does not is punished for the deeds of the entire world." (Babylonian Talmud, *Shabbat* 54b)

THERE IS little question that the Jewish tradition offers a mandate to pursue social justice. The Torah commands us to help the poor, the stranger, the orphan, and the widow (e.g., Lev. 19:9–10, 33–34; Deut. 15:4–18, 24:17–22)—those who are most vulnerable in society. The Rabbis of the Mishnah and Talmud expanded on this, demanding that every community provide a charity fund and a soup kitchen for its less fortunate members, and they spelled out the obligations of both individual Jews and Jewish communities to help not only the poor, but also the sick.

Such obligations aimed at attaining social justice are matched by the Jewish tradition's requirement for legal justice. "Justice, justice, shall you pursue" (Deut. 16:20) is a clarion call that rings out through the Jewish tradition, carrying with it many meanings. Torah demands, for example, "You shall not judge unfairly: you shall show no partiality; you shall not take bribes, for bribes blind the eyes of the discerning and upset the plea of the just" (Deut. 16:19). Further, based on the verse, "Do not stand upon the blood of your fellow" (Lev. 19:16), the Rabbis deduced that Jews who see someone drowning or being attacked by highway robbers have an obligation to take action to save that person (Sanh. 73a). Taking action to help even strangers is not, in any way, "optional." We must act justly toward others, as well as protect others from injustice.

As such, when we apply a traditional Jewish perspective to contemporary society, we find that we have a strong imperative to help those in need and that this imperative grows as our awareness does. With the help of contemporary communications, we know much more these days, not only about the needs of people in our immediate families and communities, but also about the needs of people in communities around the world. Furthermore, our increased technological abilities provide us with the means to help those that our ancestors could not have helped—those who are far away and those who are seriously ill.

Discerning how best to live out the mandate to take action, though, is not always simple. Even issues that might seem relatively easy to agree upon—for example, few would dispute that it is a good thing for the hungry to be fed and the homeless to be housed—become fraught and complex as people with different perspectives consider how best to go about achieving common goals. Debates rage over the problem of homelessness in America, for instance, with many different opinions about whether direct service or a systemic approach constitute a more effective solution (and if the latter, what systemic changes should be made, and how). Even if we choose to address such a problem through smaller-scale services, questions remain about who should pay for the services in question, and whether there should be conditions attached to or limits placed upon the services offered. How do we create a better world on the ground, and how do we navigate the obstacles that inevitably get in our way of doing so? What is the best and most just way to live out our ideals? How does one even determine which social challenges to spend his or her time and energy addressing?

Further, there are a myriad of ways to take action, to live out the mandate to create justice. For some today, social justice is pursued through philanthropy, in which righteousness (*tzedek*) is enacted primarily through charitable giving (*tzedakah*). For others, it is pursued through creating and/or participating in social justice organizations, whether or not they are Jewish; through writing or teaching about urgent issues in order to educate others and spur them to action; through organizing community service projects; through using civic channels to create or change policy that can have a dramatic impact on society as a whole; or even through doing something as deceptively simple as voting. Yet, are some of these paths preferable to others? How does each of us make an informed choice about which social justice projects best serve the people we want to help or the agenda we want to advance?

This volume will discuss social obligations in several different areas: poverty and health care; discrimination and preferential treatment; the environment; and criminal justice. As we investigate each of these topics, we will discuss both the roles of individuals and of society as a whole in dealing with the challenges these topics present, and also the requirements for social action. As we do so, readers should keep in mind the contrast between the impulse toward taking care of oneself and those in one's immediate circle and the sense of obligation to one's community.

How far do our individual and communal obligations extend? How do we decide which problems to tackle, as individuals, as communities, and even as nations? How does one individual make a difference? How do we come together with others to pursue solutions to social challenges? Finally, how can the Jewish tradition help us to respond to these critically important questions?

We hope that the sources, cases, and essays found here will help you to think through the many aspects of these tough questions about social justice, and to formulate your own responses.

CASE 1

POVERTY AND HEALTH CARE

Case Study

B ENJAMIN, a medical director for a large health management organization (HMO), wants to use his volunteer time to work for an important social cause. For instance, he's aware of the fact that 28 million people in America are classified as "working poor"—those who have one or more full-time jobs, but whose earnings are low enough to keep them below the poverty line and unable to make ends meet. He is also aware of the fact that many of these people lack adequate food, clothing, sanitation facilities, and health care, and that they often become homeless.

Yet, Benjamin has a finite amount of time and money. How can he help? Should he:

- volunteer in a soup kitchen;
- volunteer for a program that teaches literacy and job skills to teenagers and/or adults;
- work in an advocacy organization that seeks to increase government funding for the poor;
- run for political office in order to try to address social problems from inside the political establishment;
- use his time and money to support a candidate for political office who makes poverty a central issue of his or her platform;
- give donations to organizations that serve the poor.

What should each of us as individuals, and all of us as a nation, do to help alleviate poverty?

Benjamin realizes that concerns about how to help others should not only affect what he does with his spare time and money, but also what he does at work. As a medical director, he does his best to ensure that his HMO's members will receive quality care, but ultimately, he has to make sure that the HMO he works for remains solvent. This means that he must sometimes deny coverage for certain procedures or deny benefits to some subscribers of his company's HMO.

There are some 47 million Americans without health insurance, and millions more are underinsured. To what extent is this Benjamin's problem? What, if anything, should he do about this, both in his professional

3

life and in his volunteer activities? Does his responsibility change if he's working for a for-profit HMO vs. a nonprofit HMO?

Who has a duty to provide health care for the poor and the uninsured? Does the duty belong to HMOs like the one that Benjamin works for? Or does it belong to the government? Employers? Social welfare organizations? Religious institutions? Private citizens? All or none of the above?

Peter Singer, a Jewish philosopher at Princeton University, has written that Americans have a duty to tax themselves to provide basic needs like food, clothing, shelter, and health care to those in the world that have much less than they do. Do you agree that it is our civic responsibility to help alleviate poverty and assist the uninsured and underinsured? If so, to what extent?

Traditional Sources

Compiled by Uzi Weingarten and the Editors

Poverty

1. Leviticus 19:18

Love your fellow as yourself.

2. Tosefta, *Pe'ah* 4:18

Charity and kindness are equivalent to all the commandments of the Torah.

3. Babylonian Talmud, *Sotah* 14a

Rabbi Hama, son of Rabbi Hanina, said: What is the meaning of the verse, "You shall follow the Lord your God" (Deuteronomy 13:5)? … [It means that] a person should imitate the ways of the Holy Blessed One. Just as God clothes the naked … so too you should clothe the naked [poor]. The Holy Blessed One visited the sick … so too you should visit the sick. The Holy Blessed One buried the dead … so too you should bury the dead. The Holy Blessed One comforted mourners … so too you should comfort mourners …

Rabbi Samlai taught: The Torah opens with acts of kindness and closes with acts of kindness. It opens with acts of kindness, as it is written: "The Lord God made leather cloaks for Adam and his wife, and clothed them" (Genesis 3:21). It closes with acts of kindness, as it is written: "And he buried him in the valley" (Deuteronomy 34:6).

4. Babylonian Talmud, *Sukkah* 49b

Rabbi Elazar said: Charity is rewarded [by God] in accordance with the kindness that is in it.

5. Jerusalem Talmud, *Ta'anit* 21a

"I have placed my word in your mouth" (Isaiah 51:16), this refers to Torah. "And in the shadow of my hand I have covered you" (ibid.), this refers to acts of kindness. This teaches you that whoever is involved in Torah and acts of kindness merits to sit in the shadow of (i.e., next to) the Holy Blessed One.

5

6. Maimonides, *Mishneh Torah*, Laws of Gifts to the Poor 9:1–3

[1] Any city in which there are Jews, they are obligated to appoint well-known reputable people to collect charity. They make the rounds each Friday and collect from each one what is appropriate for him to give and what he has been assessed. They distribute the funds every Friday and give each needy person food that is sufficient for seven days. This is called "the fund."

[2] In addition, they appoint those who collect daily, from each courtyard, bread and various foods or fruit or money from whoever donates, and in the evening they distribute what was collected to the poor, giving each poor person his daily need. This is called "the kitchen."

[3] We never saw or heard of a Jewish community that did not have a "fund." But "the kitchen"—some places have it and some do not. The custom today is that they collect daily and distribute on Friday.

7. Maimonides (Rambam), *Mishneh Torah*, Laws of Gifts to the Poor 10:1

We are obligated to be more observant of the commandment of charity than of any other positive commandment, for charity is the sign of the righteous of the seed of Abraham, as it is written: "I have known him, so that he will command his children ... to do charity [and justice]" (Genesis 18:19).

8. Maimonides, *Mishneh Torah*, Laws of Gifts to the Poor 10:6–14

[6] One who obligates others to give has a greater reward than the one who gives ... And regarding those who collect funds for charity it is written: "And those who bring the many to righteousness [will shine] like stars" (Daniel 12:3).

[7] There are eight gradations in giving charity, each higher than the other. The highest of these, which has no superior, is one who helps a fellow Jew who became poor and offers him a gift, or a loan, or enters into a business partnership with him, or finds him a job, in order to strengthen his economic situation before he needs to ask [for help]. Concerning this, Scripture says, "You shall support him ... so that he may live with you" (Leviticus 25:35), that is, help him before he falls and needs.

[8] Less praiseworthy than this is one who gives charity to the poor and does not know to whom he gave and the recipient does not know who gave it. In this way the act of giving charity is done for its own sake.

6

This is like the Chamber of the Discreet in the Jerusalem Temple. The righteous would secretly deposit [funds], and the poor would secretly enter and be sustained (Mishnah, *Shekalim* 5:6). Another way of giving charity in this fashion is to give to the community charity fund …

[9] Less praiseworthy is when the donor knows the recipient, but the recipient does not know the donor. This is like the practice of the great Sages who would go about discreetly and toss money in the doorways of the needy …

[10] Less praiseworthy is when the needy person knows the donor but the donor does not know the recipient. This is like the practice of the great Sages who would tie coins in their shawls and let them trail behind, and the needy would come and take, so that they not have embarrassment (Babylonian Talmud, *Ketubbot* 67b).

[11] Less praiseworthy than this is personally giving a gift to someone before being asked.

[12] Less praiseworthy than this is giving after being asked.

[13] Less praiseworthy than this is giving less than is appropriate, but doing so graciously.

[14] Less praiseworthy than this is giving with sadness.

9. Jacob ben Asher (13th–14th century, Spain), *Arba Turim*, Yoreh De'ah, Chapter 251

The Torah commands that the needy of his household come first, then the poor of his city, and they, in turn, have priority over the poor of another city … Rabbi Saadia (882–942) wrote that a person is required to put his own sustenance first, and is not duty bound to give charity to others until after providing for his own. The Torah says, "And your brother shall live with you," (Leviticus 25:36), a verse that clearly establishes that your life comes first and only then the other person's [following the Babylonian Talmud, *Bava Metzi'a* 62a].

10. Maimonides, *Mishneh Torah*, Laws of Gifts to the Poor 8:15

A woman has precedence over a man regarding being fed, clothed, and [collecting funds to have her] released from prison because it is the way of a man to beg [for donations if needed] but not the way of a woman, and [thus] her embarrassment is greater.

Health Care

11. Joseph Caro (16ᵗʰ century, Spain and Israel), *Shulchan Arukh, Yoreh De'ah* **136:1, 3**

The Torah gave permission to the doctor to heal, and it is even a commandment. Even more so, it is [the commandment] of saving a life. One who prevents himself from doing so is considered to have shed blood.

One who has medications and an ill person needs them may not raise their price more than is appropriate. Not only that, but if it was an emergency and they could not find medications elsewhere and they agreed on a higher price, he is only owed what is appropriate.

12. Maimonides, *Commentary on the Mishnah,* **Nedarim 4**

This verse [the commandment to return a lost object] includes returning a person's body, for if one sees him dying and can save him, one should save him, whether physically or with money or with knowledge.

13. Eliezer Yehudah Waldenberg (20ᵗʰ century, Palestine and Israel), *Tzitz Eliezer* **5:4**

It has been enacted that in every place where Jews live, the community sets aside a fund for care of the sick. When poor people are ill and cannot afford medical expenses, the community sends them a doctor to visit them, and the medicine is paid for by the communal fund. The community gives them food appropriate for the ill, day by day, according to the directions of the doctor.

Contemporary Sources

Compiled by Steven Edelman-Blank and Julia Oestreich

Poverty

1. Felice Yeskel, "Beyond the Taboo: Talking about Class" in *The Narrow Bridge: Jewish Views on Multiculturalism,* **Marla Brettschneider, ed. (New Brunswick, NJ: Rutgers University Press, 1996), 55**

We all, even the rich, suffer in a society that generates rage, violence, illness, and despair, because of its vast inequalities. As Jews this situation should give us cause for great concern. First of all, we are overrepresented in the small group whose share of wealth continues to escalate while others' falls. Charity will not address this massive problem; *tzedakah*, justice, is what is needed. Second, when economic insecurity grows and despair increases, anger increases and violence escalates. Scapegoats are created to distract people from the real causes of their problems. Currently immigrants, welfare recipients, single mothers and gays and lesbians (who undermine the nuclear family), and people of color are the targets of misplaced rage. Jews have always been a convenient scapegoat. Given the current situation, we are vulnerable. I believe it is in our best interest as Jews to take leadership in addressing the real causes of our economic crises.

2. Joseph Telushkin, *A Code of Jewish Ethics, Vol. 2: Love Your Neighbor as Yourself* (New York: Bell Tower, 2009), 162

While the Torah places great emphasis on helping the poor, it also teaches that there will 'never cease to be needy ones in your land' (Deuteronomy 15:11). This verse should inhibit the more affluent from feeling that the problems of poverty are invariably the fault of those in need; rather, the Torah's words remind us that a certain degree of poverty is part of the human condition, an insight that should make us less judgmental of those who suffer from it.

3. Jill Jacobs, *There Shall Be No Needy: Pursuing Social Justice through Jewish Law and Tradition* (Woodstock, VT: Jewish Lights, 2009), 16. (In this passage, the author is discussing Deuteronomy 15:4–11)

A common debate among those involved in antipoverty work concerns the relative value of direct service addressing immediate needs and of advocacy or organizing addressing the need for systematic change. Advocates of direct service argue that the hungry need to be fed *today* and that the homeless need somewhere to sleep *tonight*. Those who prefer organizing or advocacy point out that soup kitchens and shelters will never make hunger and homelessness disappear, whereas structural change might wipe out these problems.

The Deuteronomic response to this debate is a refusal to take sides, or better, an insistence on both. Rather than advocate exclusively either for long-term systematic change or for short-term response to need, this passage articulates a vision that balances the pursuit of full economic justice with attention to immediate concerns. In this reading, the text in question becomes a charge to work for the structural changes that will eventually bring about the end of poverty while also meeting the pressing needs of those around us.

4. **Sidney Schwarz, *Judaism and Justice: The Jewish Passion to Repair the World* (Woodstock, VT: Jewish Lights, 2006), 191**

There is evidence to support those who would criticize the Jewish community's insularity from the problems of America's urban poor and the more general phenomenon of socioeconomic injustice in America. Some Jews do not understand why African-Americans and Hispanics need special treatment if other ethnic groups, like the Jews, succeeded in moving from immigrant poor status to middle and upper class in a matter of two or three generations. There is physical distance between where Jews now live and where the urban poor live, and the psychological distance between the two communities is even greater. In the absence of regular personal contact between the groups, there is a growing lack of understanding of the forces that lead to the persistence of urban poverty.

Health Care

5. **Elliot N. Dorff, *The Way Into Tikkun Olam* (Woodstock, VT: Jewish Lights, 2005), 156**

As much as the Jewish tradition values health care—and, as we have seen, saving lives is at the top of the Jewish agenda—health care nevertheless cannot be the sole service the community provides and must therefore be balanced against the resources expended on other social needs.

6. **Jill Jacobs, *There Shall Be No Needy: Pursuing Social Justice through Jewish Law and Tradition* (Woodstock, VT: Jewish Lights, 2009), 178**

The first step in creating a new American health care system should involve restoring community—in this case, government—control over the system. In this way, the health care system will be supported by, and accountable to the residents of the society ... this new health care system must treat all individuals as creations in the divine image, care even for those who are ostracized because of their illness or ethnicity, pay doctors enough to avoid a shortage of health care providers, and offer preventive care. Such a system has the potential to save lives, reduce differences in life expectancy among people of different economic classes, and produce a functional and equitable system for the long term.

7. **Elliot N. Dorff, "Am I My Brother's Keeper? A Jewish View on the Distribution of Health Care,"** *Conservative Judaism* **LI, No. 4 [Summer 1999], 26–27**

... the current combination in the United States of employer-related insurance plans, individual payments, and government programs like Medicaid for those who can get health care in no other way would suffice *if* that blend were effective in providing health care for everyone within our borders. The fact, however, that some forty million Americans have no health insurance whatsoever and that thousands, if not millions, lie each night on our streets and beg for food is, from a Jewish point of view, an intolerable dereliction of society's moral duty. The fact that some of those people will ultimately get health care in the most expensive way possible—namely, in the emergency room, usually when they are sickest—means that we are currently also neglecting our fiduciary responsibility to each other to spend our communal resources wisely.

8. **Lawrence D. Brown, "Health Reform in America: The Mystery of the Missing Moral Momentum,"** *Conservative Judaism* **LI, No. 4 [Summer 1999], 110**

Visible tragedies prick the national conscience. But the uninsured do not die in public view because they cannot get care. Instead, their medical ailments degenerate incrementally over the years, silently awaiting the crisis and the ride to the emergency room that proves that no one goes without. These millions of microcosmic failures to forestall human suffering, avoidable by simple acts of medical management, are invisible tragedies; they happen out of public sight, and therefore out of political mind. If the insured citizenry understood better the subtleties of coverage and access, would its antigovernmental values remain unmoved?

9. **Michael Walzer,** *Spheres of Justice: A Defense of Pluralism and Equality* **(New York: Basic Books, 1983), 89**

... no political decision has yet been made to challenge directly the system of free enterprise in medical care. And so long as that system exists, wealth will be dominant in (this part of) the sphere of security and welfare; individuals will be cared for in proportion to their ability to pay and not to their need for care ... it is clear that poverty remains a significant bar to adequate and consistent treatment.

Taking Action

10. Meir Tamari, *"With All Your Possessions": Jewish Ethics and Economic Life* (New York: The Free Press, 1987), 210–11

Perhaps the most Jewish of the underpinnings of taxation is the now universally accepted concept of society's responsibility for the needs of its members. One must bear in mind that the welfare state, with its publicly financed education, health care, and subsidies to the poor, is only a recent phenomenon amongst other nations. On the other hand, the Jewish provision of such services through the public purse, as opposed to relying on personal charity, dates back to antiquity. It must be stressed that the financing of these services bore all the hallmarks of government activity ... Irrespective of the methods chosen to finance communal needs and of the size of the communal budget, Jewish religious and legal institutions throughout the centuries maintained this vision of collective responsibility as a first principle—as axiomatic.

11. Jeffrey Dekro, "Facilitating Multicultural Progress: Community Economic Development and the American Jewish Community" in *The Narrow Bridge: Jewish Views on Multiculturalism*, Marla Brettschneider, ed. (New Brunswick, NJ: Rutgers University Press, 1996), 260

By taking note of CDFI (Community Development Financial Institutions) successes, the American Jewish community could design and implement coordinated initiatives to assist low-income community economic development nationwide. The extent of Jewish organizational and financial resources should embolden us to undertake model programs that will empower people in poor communities and permit us to fulfill the tenets of our historical values and experience. We can utilize our communal material wealth to show respect for the social and economic development of other minority groups by providing support to community-based organizations that fulfill the interests of people in those communities.

12. Joseph Telushkin, *A Code of Jewish Ethics, Vol. 2: Love Your Neighbor as Yourself* (New York: Bell Tower, 2009), 202

The fact that a significant percentage of our taxes is now used to support those in need should mitigate our feelings of guilt for giving a disproportionate percentage of our charity to our own religious, racial, or ethnic community.

Still, it is wrong to give only to our own community, for doing so—in addition to violating laws from the Torah and the Talmud—is also damaging to our character. If we donate only to Jewish causes or to individual Jews in need, we may stop seeing everyone as being equally created in God's image, and therefore worthy of our help. After all, we are all members of one race, the human race.

13. Margie Klein, "Preaching What I Practice: The Power of Jewish Organizing" in *Righteous Indignation: A Jewish Call for Justice*, Rabbi Or N. Rose, Jo Ellen Green Kaiser, and Margie Klein, eds. (Woodstock, VT: Jewish Lights, 2008), 32

When I began volunteering regularly in soup kitchens, I couldn't help but notice that week after week, I served the same people bread and soup, without offering them any path that might help them overcome their difficult circumstances. I was glad to serve, but I often felt discouraged that my volunteering was doing little to narrow the wide economic gap between our guests and me. I feared that my service did more to assuage my own liberal guilt than to create the kind of social change that would significantly impact our guests' lives. And though I learned a great deal from our guests, I had suspected that our efforts only heightened our experience of inequality, repeatedly reinforcing that they needed us, but not vice versa.

Responses

Passion, Power, and Partnership
Shmuly Yanklowitz

We are commanded to save the life of a non-Jew and to save him from harm, that if he was drowning in a river or if a stone fell upon him then we must use all of our strength and be burdened with saving him and if he was sick, we engage to heal him.
(Nahmanides [Ramban], 13th-century Spanish rabbi)[1]

I RECALL the restless nights of my first job! Between college and rabbinical school, I worked as a corporate consultant, advising employees on their benefits packages. People would call, struggling with the decision about which health insurance program would be best for them. Every choice had serious risks and the potential for immediate costs. Confined by what I perceived to be the demands of my job, I recall naively feeling restrained from sharing my empathy and spiritual concern with those seeking my help. While I knew that I was helping the workers who were coming to me, I was aware that much more needed to be done for other workers like them who were looking for guidance and support. I needed to step back to reflect upon my career path and my life direction, based upon my interests, skills, and capacity for influence.

The questions with which I struggled are, in many ways, the same questions with which Benjamin struggles in the case study and are questions that, I think, challenge many of us: Where shall I best utilize my time and energy? Should I rise in the corporate ranks in order to increase my financial net worth and then donate more to those in need? Should I spend two years volunteering in developing villages? Should I become an educator? In the past, I may have been more inclined to look to family, authority figures, and mentors to answer these difficult questions for me. At this point in my life, though, I realized that I needed to decide for myself how best to make my positive mark on the world.

---

1. Notes on *Sefer HaMitzvot*, Mitzvah 17.

I began to reflect upon the demands that Judaism places upon the ways that we invest our time, energy, and resources. I asked myself in what ways I was responsible to other people. *Acharayut* (responsibility) comes from the root *acher* (other). To take responsibility means to cultivate the "ability" to "respond" to another. This responsibility to the other is often born in a moment when no one else is present to assist. As the sage Hillel said, in a place where there is not someone (of moral courage taking responsibility), strive to be that person.[2] We each must ask ourselves: What position am I in, and how does that position provide me with special points of access that make me uniquely capable of, and thus uniquely responsible for, giving? At times the answers may be influenced by proximity (who needs me in my town), relationships (who needs me among those I know and love), and the severity of a given situation (natural disasters, for instance, can compel us to act regardless of proximity and relationships).

In my search, I found Nahmanides' argument, quoted above, to be compelling and persuasive: *One must give all of one's strength* according to one's unique position in the world. It is my contention that to actualize our potential and to fulfill our Jewish duties, we should take three critical steps: identify our core passions, build upon our power base, and cultivate partnerships for success.

Passion

The 18th-century Scottish philosopher David Hume famously argued that "it is not contrary to reason to prefer the destruction of the whole world to the scratching of my finger."[3] On some core psychological level, we might prefer to take care of the most trivial aspects of our self-interest over being proactive in addressing human suffering. A new era of activism provides us hope that this can change, but many still respond to the most pressing global issues of our age with apathy; there is a shortage of passionate, visionary justice-seekers to lead us. We need carefully deliberated giving, but even more, we need radically inspired activism and community service. We need enflamed souls who will pour their love, tears, sweat, and resources into making systemic and immediate change possible.

---

2. *Pirkei Avot* (*Ethics of the Fathers*) 2:6.
3. David Hume, *A Treatise of Human Nature*, 2:128 (London: J.M. Dent, 1911).

The *Shema* commands us to serve (via love of God) with all of our resources *(uvchol meodekha)*. The medieval philosopher Maimonides explains the virtues of excess in ethical pursuits:

> The hasid [pious person] is the wise man who has inclined some-what to an extreme in his ethical attributes ... and his deeds are greater than his wisdom. Therefore he is called a hasid, in the sense of excess, because exaggeration in a matter is called hesed [loving-kindness] ...[4]

Following the path of Jewish piety, we are asked to be radically excessive in our healing of the world. We must not only invigorate our general commitments to altruism, human rights, and activism, but also find our unique passions, and then pursue them in service to the world.

We cannot evaluate our social justice options using conventions or religious dogma. Rather, we should follow our consciences and our reasoning about how to make life better for others and join communities that are striving to improve the world in similar ways. We must create open spaces of discourse so that our identities and our lives can inspire responsibility; this is how we become enthusiastic and committed to our work. When we choose projects that feel right and speak to our souls, we ensure that our commitments to them will be sustainable, that we will be able to invest in them in a deeper, more lasting way. When our souls are enflamed with passion for the causes we choose to address, we can be moved to the kind of excess Jewish tradition praises in order to serve those who cry out to us.

Power

As mentioned above, Nahmanides argued that when a life circumstance puts someone in a position of influence, he or she is obligated to use that power to save others. The great 16th-century Jewish legal code, the *Shulchan Arukh*, even stated that one must "expose oneself to possible danger *(safek sakkanah)* to save a human life."[5] In his comments on this issue, the 20th-century rabbi Shlomo Zalman Auerbach argued:

---

4. *Commentary on the Mishnah, Avot* 5:6.
5. Joseph Caro, *Kesef Mishnah, Hilkhot Rotzeach* 1:14; Joseph Caro, *Hoshen Mishpat* 426.

In relation to the obligation to pay the costs of saving the life of a sick person who is in danger of dying: From the straightforward reading of [the Talmud, Tractate] Sanhedrin 73a we see that one is obligated to do everything to save him, and if not, one transgresses the negative commandment: Do not stand idly by the blood of your neighbor.[6]

The problem is that each of us must operate under constraints of time, money, location, and relationships—sadly, we can't help everyone. Given these limitations, what methods are most appropriate in our attempt to make the world a more just, safe, moral, and holy place, and who are the needy whom we should make a priority in doing that work? When we consider the amount of people in the world who need our help, we can get overwhelmed.

We should therefore emphasize methods of social action that effect the most change, while also promoting multiple approaches in order to make use of the diverse talents and positions held by individuals within the Jewish community. Some people choose to serve as great philanthropists, some as community organizers and lobbyists, while others are social workers or clergy. We must encourage all of these options as means to build a powerful base of partnership while adhering to the famous principle of Jewish education, "chanoch la-na'ar al pi darko,"[7] which means that education should be based on the particular path of each student. After identifying our core values and concerns, we must learn to use our spheres of influence and skills in the most effective way possible. If we are well-connected to power or to wealth, or armed with a particular kind of knowledge, these factors should be taken into account.

We must also be in touch with our environment. At times, we may be placed in a position of power when the need for action is immediate. The Talmud teaches in the name of Rabbi Nachum Ish Gam Zo:

A poor man came and stood before me on the road, and said to me, "My teacher, sustain me (give me something to eat)!" I responded to him: "Wait until I unload some food from the donkey." I did not have

---

6. Shlomo Zalman Auerbach, *Minchat Shlomo*, Vol. 2, 86:4.
7. Proverbs 22:6.

a chance to unload the donkey before his soul departed (he died of hunger). I went and fell on my face [fell into depression based on my insensitivity at having not prevented this man's death at the chance I was given].[8]

We are all confronted with these chances. But sometimes even decisions made with the best intentions don't necessarily have the greatest effect.

Peter Singer, a moral consequentialist,[9] suggested that the morally superior path is a life of asceticism in which we renounce everything beyond our basic needs, using whatever else we have to donate to the less fortunate; but I would argue that this is not likely to be a lifestyle that affects the most change in the long run. Such a life would not enable ongoing, sustainable giving or produce more creative possibilities for contribution. Donating the majority of our income and wealth, as Singer has advocated, should not be done at the expense of creating change in other necessary ways. Giving money is only one way to contribute; we can also offer our time, social entrepreneurship, political influence, and knowledge. A CEO may, in fact, be able to create more significant change by reforming his or her company's labor practices than he or she could by merely writing a check. There are power dynamics in every relationship,[10] and we should look at situations holistically to assess where each of us can best use our own power for positive social change.

Partnership
Though we can best contribute in areas where we have the most potential for influence and where we have the most passion to make a difference, we cannot do it alone. We must work in partnership with our community, with the population we are hoping to impact (that may or may not be in our community), with co-religionists, and with experts. Coming

---

8. Babylonian Talmud, *Taanit* 21a.
9. A moral consequentalist is not merely interested in the cultivation of virtue or in preserving rights. The consequences of any individual act can be greater than intelligence can acknowledge and thus all moral deliberation must acknowledge this factor. The question is not whether it is right to do X at this moment, but how doing X might impact all parties in the future.
10. See *Michel Foucault: Politics, Philosophy, Culture*, Lawrence Kreitzman, ed. (New York: Routledge, 1988).

face-to-face with others is a necessary element of working for social change. Even when we have limited time and resources to contribute, we should nonetheless ensure that, at a minimum, we seek to maintain personal relationships with those we want to help, so that we may better understand their needs on their terms.

And yet, there is room for self-interest, even in the quest for partnership. The influential 20th-century rabbi Joseph B. Soloveitchik wrote:

> What one is longing for is his own self-fulfillment, which he believes he will find in his union with the other person. The emotion leaves its inner abode in order to find not the "you" but the "I" … It only indicates that, because of self-interest, the person is committed to a state of mind which, regardless of one's self-centeredness, promotes goodwill and unites people.[11]

Self-interest, concomitant with a desire to create good, should not be condemned.

In addition to supporting each other, we are also obligated to challenge each other. The Rabbis expected that we would hold others in our sacred communities accountable for our collective responsibility. The Talmud says,

> Whoever has the power to protest against members of his household but does not protest is punished for the transgressions of the members of his household. Against the people of his town, but does not, is punished for the deeds of those in his town. Against the entire world and does not is punished for the deeds of the entire world.[12]

Jewish ethics is, of course, not only about avoiding wrongdoing. Rather, we have a greater mandate to go beyond the ethics of the "do no harm" principle and the responsibility to repair the world from its brokenness. We are asked to partner with others to help meet our potential for moral leadership. As a nation, we are commanded to commit to being *laasot tzedakah u'mishpat*—a nation enacting justice.[13] Setting positive

---

11. Joseph B. Soloveitchik, *Out of the Whirlwind, A Theory of Emotions* (New York: KTAV, 2003), 200.
12. Babylonian Talmud, *Shabbat* 54b.
13. Genesis 18:19.

examples that cultivate leadership in our communities is vital to the Jewish moral enterprise and to the creation of a vibrant, just society.

Talmud Torah, the study of Torah, is a central responsibility for Jews; and yet, addressing communal needs is considered to have equal weight in our tradition.[14] What makes Jewish education matter is not only that it demands high standards and intellectual rigor, but also that it challenges us to make a greater commitment to justice, charity, service, and volunteering. The Rabbis explained that one cannot be content and comfortable while others suffer. Rather, they argued, "At a time when the community is steeped in distress, a person should not say: 'I will go to my house and eat and drink, and peace be upon you, my soul.'"[15]

While we may live in a country in which over 47 million people lack medical insurance, we also live in a world in which over 2 billion people out of a global population of 6 billion not only live without medical insurance, but also make barely enough money to sustain themselves and their families. Because poverty and disease are spreading throughout many regions of the world, there is too much at stake for us to act as if we live or work in a vacuum. The Jewish community, despite the many differences among its members, must unite on a global scale to address these pressing issues.

Conclusion

To make the greatest possible contribution to the world, each of us must take a *cheshbon hanefesh* (self-accounting) of our spheres of influence and personal callings. When we act on the issues about which we are the most personally passionate, while contributing where we have the most potential for influence, we ensure that our giving will have the greatest possible sustainability and impact. To be sure, there are traditional basic minimum prescriptions for *tzedakah*, core responsibilities to family and community, and hierarchies of Jewish values. The 19th-century rabbi Moshe Sofer, however, maintained that a very great need overrides

---

14. Joseph Caro, *Shulchan Arukh, Yoreh De'ah* 93:4.
15. Babylonian Talmud, *Ta'anit* 11a.

the traditional hierarchy of priorities altogether.[16] Another 19th-century rabbi, Yechiel Michel Epstein (also known as the *Arukh HaShulchan*), similarly argued that everyone—not only the relatives and neighbors of those in need—must give to poor people.[17]

There are no adequate absolute prescriptions that can help us choose between lending our efforts to rescuing the people of Darfur or fighting malaria, to helping the elderly or feeding malnourished newborns, to assisting with immediate disaster relief or creating sustainable development, to offering services to those lacking health care or contributing to AIDS research. And yet, we can analyze the power we have, assess our skill sets, and identify our core convictions. These steps will help us to understand where we might best contribute and organize for effective change through diverse partnerships. For each of us to realize our full potential in the project of repairing the world, we must measure the efficacy of our work. Together as a Jewish community, may we reach new heights in creating concrete change that brings dignity to all human beings and peace to all corners of the earth!

---

16. "There is something about this that is very difficult for me because if we understand these words literally—that some groups take priority over others—that implies that there is no requirement to give to groups lower on the hierarchy. And it is well known that every wealthy person has many poor relatives (and all the more so every poor person) so it will happen that a poor person without any rich relatives will die of hunger. And how could this possibly be? So it seems clear to me that the correct interpretation is that everyone, whether rich or poor, must also give to poor people who are not relatives" (Caro, *Shulchan Arukh, Yoreh De'ah* 151:4).
17. Yechiel Michel Epstein, *Arukh Hashulchan* 251:4.

Health Care for the Homeless: An Interview with Lillian Gelberg

Elliot N. Dorff

The following is a transcript of an interview that Elliot Dorff conducted with Dr. Lillian Gelberg in Los Angeles on October 22, 2009.

Public Health and the Homeless

Elliot Dorff: Let's talk a bit about your background relative to this case.

Lillian Gelberg: I am a physician with specialty training in family medicine and public health/health services research. As part of my family medicine residency at the Montefiore Residency Program in Social Medicine, I worked in the South Bronx, and during my social medicine elective, worked with the Venice Family Clinic in Los Angeles as they were setting up their first program to provide health care for the homeless. I did a needs assessment of the homeless community to assist the Venice Family Clinic with designing clinical programs for homeless persons.

Then, as part of my fellowship (post-residency program) in the VA/UCLA Robert Wood Johnson Foundation Clinical Scholar's Program, I conducted a large community-based survey to identify health needs and barriers to obtaining health care for the homeless population on the west side of Los Angeles. We considered health broadly, as defined by the World Health Organization (WHO), to include physical, mental, and social well-being. We identified all problem areas, including dental care, nutritional care, housing and social service problems, and violence. We went out with six volunteer medical and undergraduate students to all areas where homeless persons congregated on the west side—the beaches, parks, free meal programs, bus stations, and emergency shelters—and conducted medical histories, physical examinations, and blood testing of over 500 homeless people.

I drew blood on everybody as the trained phlebotomist. We did whatever aspects of the physical examination we could do from head to toe, given the limitation of not having privacy. We set up mats on the beach and performed nutritional assessments and dental evaluations, looked at people's feet and skin, assessed their vision and gait, and measured people's height and weight. It was one of the most amazing experiences I've ever had.

Then I obtained grants from various institutes of the National Institutes of Health (NIH) to help me study the epidemiology and access to medical care for homeless people, regarding women's health, Hepatitis B and C, tuberculosis, HIV, high blood pressure, vision problems, and dermatological and podiatry problems. We conducted community-based probability surveys, developed methodologies for lay people to conduct medical screenings to identify unmet needs for medical care among various populations, designed brief interventions conducted in clinical environments and in the field to promote healthy lifestyles, and referred those who had unmet medical needs to primary care at community health centers. We identified cost-effective methods for screening homeless people to identify health problems, and for referring them to get their health care needs met.

We found that virtually none of the homeless people we interviewed had received treatment for Hepatitis C, and yet close to 30% were infected with this virus. Many health care providers and planners believed that it was not a good use of resources to treat homeless people for Hepatitis C, citing such reasons as the high cost, long duration (6–12 months), and often disabling side effects of treatment.

My colleagues and I set up a primary care-run Hepatitis C clinic downtown in an established community health center in the Skid Row area of Los Angeles. The clinic provided hepatitis C treatment integrated with medical and social services for health, self-care management, housing, mental health, and substance abuse. Participating in the integrated Hepatitis C clinic has given the clients comprehensive care and a staff devoted to their healing and recovery. Indeed, the homeless adhere to the Hepatitis C treatment, even though it is long. Further, the services of the integrated clinic are devoted to their recovery, giving them hope and enabling them to turn their lives around. This is an example of how care that is acceptable, achievable, and compassionate can be provided with sustained support.

I have also aimed to develop sustainable health promotion tools and programs for low-income patients of community health centers, where we are conducting randomized controlled clinical trials on the primary prevention of obesity, chronic disease, and mental illness by focusing on healthy lifestyles. We call it our "Healthy Choices" program. The program provides education and counseling to assist patients in reaching their goals for increasing healthy eating and physical activity, reducing sedentary behaviors, and controlling their weight. Another of our community-based clinical trials aims to reduce substance abuse before it causes alcohol and drug dependence and permanent brain changes.

What Benjamin Should Do

ED: So in the case study, how should Benjamin invest his time and money?

LG: If Benjamin is the medical director of an HMO who wants to volunteer his time for social causes, I would suggest that he volunteer in a soup kitchen and take colleagues and medical students with him because they will see firsthand that people who are experiencing homelessness are real people, they are not frightening and they are no different from all of us. This kind of experience is humbling and will enable them to see what is going on in real life. My mentor understood the importance of first-hand experience. Before he allowed me to do anything with the homeless population, he sent me out to the beaches on the West Side just to learn about who the homeless people were. I went with my little pad of paper and just started having conversations with them.

ED: You would have Benjamin do that, rather than spend his time organizing people to advocate to government officials on behalf of the homeless?

LG: The two activities are not mutually exclusive. Benjamin is already working at an HMO, so he could be an advisor on issues related to health care, using reports prepared by his organization or by other advocacy organizations to influence health care legislation, planning, and policy.

ED: What about other possible uses of Benjamin's time and energy?

LG: Benjamin's skills and training in the area of health care management are invaluable to the work needed to improve the health of the underserved. It might not be the best use of Benjamin's expertise to provide vocational skills training to homeless persons to help them find jobs and permanent housing.

Setting Priorities

ED: What should be our priorities, as individuals and as a nation, for working to alleviate poverty? In other words, if you had a magic wand, what would be the *first* thing that you would do?

LG: Every person should have permanent housing that he or she can afford, and that housing should be safe and healthy, with running water, heat, working sanitation, and intact windows. Jobs should be available so that everyone able to work can get work. If they are not employable, we should train them for employment. If, however, a person is ill or disabled, he or she should be supported. We should also support poor neighborhoods and build better environments, strengthening the social fabric of our community so that better choices can be made.

One way of looking at how to provide housing and social services to the homeless population is called the "Housing First" approach. This new approach is now being used because we have discovered that the provision of permanent housing is the most important ingredient in helping homeless people become housed and stay housed. Mental health treatment, drug treatment, and other interventions have a much better chance of having a sustained affect if a homeless person has a place to live other than an emergency shelter. How can a person keep a job if he or she has to search for shelter; does not have a place to sleep at night that is quiet and safe from violence and theft; does not have a place to store his or her belongings during the day, since most emergency shelters are only open at night; and does not have a place to bathe?

Thus, we need to provide homeless people with stable permanent housing as a first step. If they have a drug and alcohol problem, we should use the harm reduction approach in their recovery process, stabilizing them in secure, long-term housing with built-in supportive services. This readies the clients for a program that fosters the development of self-esteem and trust, reduces their alcohol or drug use, encourages them to seek mental health treatment, and helps them obtain life skills and vocational counseling and training.

Another key issue is to prevent the poor from spiraling downward into homelessness. The very low-income population and homeless population are in many ways the same population, as there is a lot of movement back and forth between being homeless and being low-income and marginally housed. Ideally, we try to maintain people in marginal housing to keep them from becoming homeless. If people are homeless for too long they can get used to it. Over time, the experience of being homeless is not so shocking anymore; they find out where to get food, shelter, and medical care, and make friends on the streets.

We need to stabilize low-income people, but there is no one recipe that will work for all. Mental health and other interventions need to be targeted to the needs of the individual. One person may need a life coach that she or he can bounce ideas off of indefinitely. Another person may need short-term mental health care or help coping with, or escaping from, domestic violence. Still others may need life skills training because they may not know how to maintain a job, save money, balance their expenses, make hard decisions, or parent their children. And then there are some people who are newly impoverished and just need to earn a living. It is critical to give homeless persons a *parnasah* (livelihood), a job they can do to support themselves. If they cannot earn their own *parnasah*, the government may need to chip in to support them.

I believe that it is the responsibility of all of us to take care of each other. As Jews, we are supposed to give *tzedakah* (charity). This is not only an individual obligation, but also a communal and societal obligation.

Changing the System

ED: Benjamin realizes that these concerns should affect not only what he does with his spare time and money, but also what he does at work. How should he balance providing access to health care for those who need it, even if they are not members of the HMO for which he works, with the HMO's need to remain solvent?

LG: Every organization should set aside a certain amount of money to care for the poor. This is *tzedakah*, to which everybody should be contributing. There are a lot of really smart minds who could come together and figure out a good system that would be sustainable and that would incentivize people to provide quality care accessible to all, regardless of income.

Basic, quality health care should be available to everybody, so we need to figure out what basic insurance coverage is required for good health and adequate health care. What is the right thing to do here? I don't know that there is one perfect system out there, but we have to start somewhere. We need to develop incentives for those, like Benjamin, working in the health care system to do the right thing: that is, to insure that there is coverage for essential medical care, that is of high quality and is tailored to the individual patient's needs.

The Reach and the Limits of Responsibility
Jill Jacobs

A BRAHAM JOSHUA Heschel famously wrote, "Few are guilty, but all are responsible."[1] That is to say, only a small number of people actively cause violence, but all members of society assume responsibility for inaction in the face of such violence. This statement rings true for many of the major events of the 20th and 21st centuries. How can we forgive the world for standing by during the Holocaust, or more recently, for the inaction of so many during the genocide in Darfur?

But few events carry the moral clarity of genocide. While it is easy to criticize the failure to respond to mass murder, it is much harder to assign blame for everyday lapses in confronting injustice. By virtue of earning and spending money, eating, and simply living in the world, all of us bear some responsibility for low wages and difficult working conditions, environmental degradation, and the continued poverty of millions of people. Should we be held responsible for the labor practices of the restaurants where we eat, the environmental practices of companies in which our banks invest, or the political causes to which the owners of our local stores contribute? What if the connection is twice removed? For example, what if I buy a cup of coffee from a local café whose owner then invests money in a mutual fund that invests in tobacco? Do I then share responsibility for the millions of people who die of tobacco-related illnesses each year? Or is the locus of responsibility too far removed from me?

The Implications of Benjamin's Dilemma
There is no doubt that Judaism values human life above almost all else. God declares human beings to be created in the divine image. Accordingly, Jewish law permits the violation of virtually any law in order to rescue a person from death. For instance, doctors and medical residents who observe Shabbat regularly tend to patients and respond to emergencies on Shabbat, doing work ordinarily not permitted on the day of rest. Those who are ill and likely to put themselves in danger by fasting are allowed, or even required, to eat on Yom Kippur and on other fast days.

---

1. Abraham Joshua Heschel, *The Prophets* (New York: Harper Perennial Classics, 2001), 19.

Does the obligation to protect human life still apply, however, when death is neither certain nor probable? And does this responsibility fall only on the person who is capable of saving a person's life directly, or does it also fall on those with indirect involvement? In the case study, Benjamin has some authority for determining who receives health care claim coverage and who does not. The potential implications of his decision are huge: a diabetic denied coverage for care may wait until she goes into insulin shock to seek emergency care, rather than visit a doctor regularly for health maintenance. A person who lacks insurance coverage may suffer a medical crisis and find him- or herself saddled with hospital debts likely to send him or her into bankruptcy. On the other hand, some people who lack medical insurance will be lucky enough not to get sick, or will find their way to a free clinic or some other charitable care facility. When denying coverage to an applicant, Benjamin cannot predict with certainty whether that decision will lead to death, serious illness, or a financial crisis, or will simply be an annoyance for the individual concerned.

It would be easy for us to say that Benjamin should approve every application for coverage for a procedure, treatment, or medication that comes his way. This approach would guarantee that no one ever died or lost his or her savings as a result of his rulings. But Benjamin is not the CEO of his insurance company, and he is unlikely to keep his job for long if he grants coverage for all claims. Then he will be unemployed and people will keep being denied coverage from his former company. Furthermore, Jewish law forbids employees from stealing, even indirectly, from their employers. In approving coverage beyond company guidelines for applicants likely to cost the company large amounts of money, Benjamin would certainly cut into the company's profits, and might even be terminated.

Like Benjamin, many of us wonder about the direct and indirect effects of our actions. A heightened consciousness of the potential global effects of our consumer, investment, and workplace practices has led many of us to make small choices that we hope will have some effect on global systems. We may bring our own bags to the grocery store with the intention of reducing waste, avoid buying clothing made in sweatshops in the hope of ending the use of child labor, or invest our money in companies whose values align with ours. We know that we are not guilty of amassing large amounts of waste, or of hiring children to work for us, but we

28

see ourselves as complicit in allowing destructive systems to continue. Yet, it will take years, or possibly decades, to know whether our individual choices will have an impact on the world as a whole, and most of us are unlikely to meet the individuals who are indirectly affected by our choices.

Benjamin, on the other hand, lacks the luxury of distance. He has the name, address, medical history, and other personal information of each person to whom he may deny coverage. His job entails making educated guesses about whether these individuals are likely to become ill, and he therefore can predict with some accuracy who will suffer most from his decisions. But he also knows the financial situation of his own company, and he understands that lenience will possibly lead to the financial distress of the business.

Benjamin and the Gladiator

Modern health care practices are extraordinarily complicated and involve dozens of parties, from patients and HMOs to drug companies and government agencies. Classical Jewish sources on health care and related issues generally assume a much simpler system, in which the major players are the patient, the doctor, and the general community. Still, these texts capture the wisdom of hundreds of years of thinking about the best way to maintain a society that supports the well-being of its citizens. Though traditional texts may not speak precisely to our current situation, they offer insights that can help us to approach today's health care issues.

I will begin with one 2nd- or 3rd-century source that, on the face of it, has nothing to do with health care. This text considers whether Jews may attend Roman gladiator matches, which often ended with the death of the losing gladiator. It quotes two opinions on the matter. The first rabbi quoted forbids attendance at such events on the basis that the audience effectively participates in murder by sanctioning brutal and deadly fights. A second rabbi, however, notes that spectators at these events sometimes vote on whether the losing gladiator should live or die. He therefore concludes that Jews may attend these events for the purpose of voting to save a life.[2]

In some ways, Benjamin's situation parallels that of the audience member of a gladiator competition. He has some power to save the lives of the

---

2. Tosefta, *Avodah Zarah* 2:7.

people whose insurance claims he considers, but he does not have absolute power. His superiors are likely to override his decision on certain applications, and even a person who receives health care with coverage from Benjamin's company may fall ill or die. On the flip side, a person whose insurance claim Benjamin denies may find insurance elsewhere, or may even lead a long, healthy life without coverage. Like the audience members at a gladiator competition, Benjamin risks contributing to a death if he participates in the system, but he has no chance of preventing such a death if he opts out by quitting his job.

Staging a public protest, either in the course of a gladiator fight or as an employee of an HMO, will likely lead to punishment—in one case through ejection from the arena, and in the other case through dismissal from a job. In both instances, those whom the system is most likely to hurt are those with the least power. Although some gladiators volunteered for their jobs, many were slaves or citizens of conquered nations, and others had little choice but to succumb to the will of the Roman rulers. Though not slaves or official second-class citizens, people who lack health insurance are likely to have less money or power than other members of society and are more likely to be totally dependent on the decisions of the health care bureaucracy.

In different ways, both Benjamin and the spectator at a gladiator fight find themselves trapped in a society that ultimately fails to guarantee the health and safety of its members, and specifically of its most vulnerable members. Outside of using their own limited power to prevent individual deaths in the immediate future, both should also look for ways to create a more equitable society in the long term.

Communal Responsibility

Since the earliest times, Jewish communities have established *tzedakah* funds for the care of the poor. Each member of the community is obligated to contribute to these funds, and anyone in need may draw from them. In addition to paying for food, clothing, and other necessities, some of these funds have been traditionally allocated for health care costs. Rabbi Moshe Waldenberg (1915–2006), one of the major 20th-century authorities on medical ethics, commented:

> It has been enacted that in every place in which Jews live, the community sets aside a fund for care of the sick. When poor people are ill and cannot afford medical expenses, the community sends them

a doctor to visit them, and the medicine is paid for by the communal fund. The community gives them food appropriate for the ill, day by day, according to the directions of the doctor.[3]

In the system that Waldenberg describes, unlike in the current American system, the entire community shares responsibility for the care of the sick. Everyone in the community contributes to the fund to care for the sick, and the community ensures that those who are ill receive doctors, medicine, food, and whatever else may be necessary for recovery. Community members know that if they fall ill and find themselves unable to afford medical care, the community will step up to support them. This system therefore produces a commitment from each member of the community to invest in the well-being of all other members, as well as an incentive to distribute funds in a way that serves the greatest number of people possible.

In contrast, an HMO is accountable to no one but its stakeholders, some of whom may receive health care coverage from the HMO and some of whom may receive health care coverage elsewhere. However, the people who contribute to the financial health of the HMO—largely those insured by it—have no say in how the HMO determines who receives coverage or which doctors or procedures are covered. Unlike the members of a community, who appoint their leaders and *tzedakah* administrators, the members of an HMO do not elect the CEO or the board members of the company. As a for-profit venture, an HMO must ultimately be more concerned about income and about the demands of its stakeholders than about the health of the community as a whole.

A national health care system would more closely approach Waldenberg's description of a community in which each person takes responsibility for the health of every other person. In a national system, all citizens contribute—in the form of tax dollars—to a communal fund. Citizens also elect the political leadership, who in turn appoint specific cabinet members and program administrators, all of whom are also theoretically accountable to the voters. Such a system has more of a chance than an HMO-based system to create a community in which each person feels invested in the well-being of other members of society, and in which there can be a communal discussion of how to best allocate resources in order to maintain the health of as many people as possible.

---

3. Eliezer Yehudah Waldenberg, *Tzitz Eliezer* 5:4.

As I write this piece, the United States Congress is debating a health care bill that could guarantee coverage for most Americans and ban practices such as denying insurance to high-risk patients. If Benjamin wishes to ultimately free himself and his colleagues from the unenviable task of denying health care coverage for some insurance claims and for applicants whose policies do not have a waiver for "pre-existing conditions," he might consider volunteering for one of the many advocacy organizations working to pass this bill. Through this effort, he would be responding to Heschel's challenge to take personal responsibility for the failings of society.

CASE 2

❧

DISCRIMINATION AND PREFERENTIAL TREATMENT

Case Study

Discrimination and Preferential Treatment

1. Discrimination

Discrimination occurs in several forms. Sometimes, it is legally encoded, as in Jim Crow legislation of the late 19th and early-to-mid 20th century, (restrictive covenants that barred Jews and other groups from buying homes in certain areas) and in current laws banning same-sex marriages.

Is it ever right to discriminate by law against a minority within the population? If so, for what reasons? For example, is it appropriate that only men are allowed to serve in military combat? Is it right that only people born in the United States may run for President? What does "equal treatment under the law" as required by the 14th Amendment of the U.S. Constitution mean if the country has laws that treat some people unequally?

Sometimes, discrimination that is not codified legally occurs socially. For example, overweight people encounter discrimination in many ways in their day-to-day life, due to a general bias in contemporary society. This may affect their ability to receive good customer service, fair evaluations as potential adoptive or foster parents, and appropriate and unbiased medical care, as well as their ability to get access to suitable clothing. How should we, as individuals and as a society, deal with biases that are impossible to ban by law?

2. Hate Crimes

Sometimes, prejudice takes on violent forms. This has included everything from the pogroms of Europe and lynchings in the American South to more recent attacks on, and sometimes murders of, gays, lesbians, and transgender people.

Should such crimes be prosecuted as hate crimes, meaning that the perpetrators face harsher penalties than they normally would? Does a motive of hate require that an assault and/or homicide be prosecuted as having aggravating circumstances?

3. Affirmative Action

President Lyndon Johnson instituted affirmative action clauses in government contracts in the 1960s in order to address the disadvantages that African-Americans faced in the job market—a result of long-standing discrimination they suffered throughout American history. In addition, through the 1990s, many colleges and professional schools set aside places for African-Americans and Hispanics in their entering classes, even when the admitted students may have been less academically qualified than others who had applied. The latter policy resulted in several lawsuits against the University of California-Davis, University of Michigan, and Columbia University that ultimately reached the U.S. Supreme Court. In those cases, the Supreme Court drew vague lines as to what universities may do to attract people of color to their schools. More recently, universities have engaged in similar practices to attract women to graduate programs in science and men to undergraduate liberal arts programs.

How does one judge issues of "fairness" presented by affirmative action? Think about the result of affirmative action programs for individuals, both those in groups given preferential treatment and those not in such groups. Even if affirmative action, as it has been practiced in the past, has flaws, is some sort of program warranted to address past injustices?

Traditional Sources

Compiled by Uzi Weingarten and the Editors

Discrimination

1. Genesis 1:27

And God created man in His image, in the image of God He created him; male and female He created them.

2. Deuteronomy 17:14–15

If, after you have entered the land that the LORD your God has assigned to you, and taken possession of it and settled in it, you decide, "I will set a king over me, as do all the nations about me," you shall be free to set a king over yourself, one chosen by the LORD your God. Be sure to set as king over yourself one of your own people; you must not set a foreigner over you, one who is not your kinsman.

3. Numbers 15:15–16

There shall be one law for you and for the resident stranger; it shall be a law for all time throughout the ages. You and the stranger shall be alike before the LORD; the same ritual and the same rule shall apply to you and to the stranger who resides among you.

4. Babylonian Talmud, *Gittin* 61a

Our Rabbis taught: We sustain the non-Jewish poor with the Jewish poor, visit the non-Jewish sick with the Jewish sick, and bury the non-Jewish dead with the Jewish dead, for the sake of peace.

5. Babylonian Talmud, *Ta'anit* 20b

[A sage was returning] from his master's house, riding on the donkey along the riverbank, and feeling haughty because he had learned much Torah. A particularly ugly person chanced by and said to him: "Peace unto you, Master!" [The Sage] did not return his greeting, and [instead] said to him: "How ugly is that person! Are all your townsfolk as ugly as you?" [The person] said to him: "I don't know. However, go and say to the Craftsman who made me: 'How ugly is this vessel You made!'" Seeing that he had sinned, [the sage] dismounted from the donkey, prostrated himself before the man, and said: "I humble myself before you. Forgive me!"

6. Midrash, *Bereshit Rabbah* 24:7, elaborating on Genesis 5:1

Rabbi Akiva taught: "Love your neighbor as yourself" (Leviticus 19:18): this is a great principle in the Torah. Therefore, do not say: "Since I was demeaned, let my fellow be demeaned as well, since I was cursed let my fellow be cursed as well."

Rabbi Tanhuma said: If you do this, know Whom you are demeaning, [since] "In the image of God He made him" (Genesis 5:1).

Hate Crimes

7. Deuteronomy 19:4

Now this is the case of the manslayer who may flee there (i.e., to the cities of refuge) and live: one who has killed another unwittingly, without having been his enemy in the past.

8. Deuteronomy 19:11–12

If, however, a person who is the enemy of another lies in wait for him and sets upon him and strikes him a fatal blow and then flees to one of these towns, the elders of his town shall have him brought back from there and shall hand him over to the blood-avenger to be put to death.

9. 1 Kings 21: 1–19

[The following events] occurred sometime afterward: Naboth the Jezreelite owned a vineyard in Jezreel, adjoining the palace of King Ahab of Samaria. Ahab said to Naboth, "Give me your vineyard, so that I may have it as a vegetable garden, since it is right next to my palace. I will give you a better vineyard in exchange; or, if you prefer, I will pay you the price in money." But Naboth replied, "The LORD forbid that I should give up to you what I have inherited from my fathers!" Ahab went home dispirited and sullen because of the answer that Naboth the Jezreelite had given him: "I will not give up to you what I have inherited from my fathers!" He lay down on his bed and turned away his face, and he would not eat. His wife Jezebel came to him and asked him, "Why are you so dispirited that you won't you eat?" So he told her, "I spoke to Naboth the Jezreelite and proposed to him, 'Sell me your vineyard for money, or if you prefer, I'll give you another vineyard in exchange;' but he answered, 'I will not give my vineyard to you.'"

His wife Jezebel said to him, "Now is the time to show yourself king over Israel. Rise and eat something, and be cheerful; I will get the vineyard of Naboth the Jezreelite for you."

So she wrote letters in Ahab's name and sealed them with his seal, and sent the letters to the elders and the nobles who lived in the same town with Naboth. In the letters she wrote as follows: "Proclaim a fast and seat Naboth at the front of the assembly. And seat two scoundrels opposite him, and let them testify against him: 'You have reviled God and king!' Then take him out and stone him to death."

His townsmen—the elders and nobles who lived in his town—did as Jezebel had instructed them, just as was written in the letters she had sent them: They proclaimed a fast and seated Naboth at the front of the assembly. Then the two scoundrels came and sat down opposite him; and the scoundrels testified against Naboth publicly as follows: "Naboth has reviled God and king." Then they took him outside the town and stoned him to death. Word was sent to Jezebel: "Naboth has been stoned to death." As soon as Jezebel heard that Naboth had been stoned to death, she said to Ahab, "Go and take possession of the vineyard which Naboth the Jezreelite refused to sell you for money; for Naboth is no longer alive, he is dead." When Ahab heard that Naboth was dead, Ahab set out for the vineyard of Naboth the Jezreelite to take possession of it.

Then the word of the LORD came to Elijah the Tishbite: "Go down and confront King Ahab of Israel, who [resides] in Samaria. He is now in Naboth's vineyard; he has gone down there to take possession of it. Say to him, 'Thus said the LORD: Would you murder and take possession? Thus said the LORD: In the very place where the dogs lapped up Naboth's blood, the dogs will lap up your blood too.'"

Preferential Treatment

10. Deuteronomy 14:2

For you are a people consecrated to the LORD your God: and the LORD your God chose you from among all other peoples on earth to be His treasured people.

11. Babylonian Talmud, *Gittin* 11b

Rabbi Yochanan says: One who seizes on behalf of a debtor, in a situation where he creates a loss for others, [the debtor] has not acquired.

Note: The point of this teaching is that one may not "seize" for the benefit of one party at the expense of the other.

12. Maimonides (Rambam), *Mishneh Torah*, Laws of Lenders and Borrowers 20:2

One who seizes [an item] on behalf of a debtor, in a situation where the owner of the item has a debt to others, the debtor did not acquire the object. If the owner does not have a debt to others, the debtor did acquire the object.

13. Babylonian Talmud, *Bava Metzi'a* 71a

Rabbi Yosef taught, "If you lend money to my people, to the poor among you, do not act as a creditor toward them" (Exodus 22:24). In the case of a Jew and a non-Jew, the Jew takes precedence; a poor person and a wealthy person, the poor person takes precedence; a poor person of your own city and a poor person of another city, the poor person of your city takes precedence.

14. Shabbat Morning Amidah Liturgy

The people Israel shall observe Shabbat, to maintain it as an everlasting covenant throughout all generations. It is a sign between Me and the people Israel for all time … You have not granted this day, LORD our God, to other peoples of the world, nor have You granted it, our King, as a heritage to idolaters. Nor do those outside the covenant know its rest, which You have given lovingly to the people Israel, Your beloved descendants of Jacob. May the people who make the seventh day holy find satisfaction and delight in Your generosity.

Contemporary Sources

Compiled by Steven Edelman-Blank and Julia Oestreich

Discrimination

1. Elliot N. Dorff, *The Way Into Tikkun Olam (Repairing the World)* (Woodstock, VT: Jewish Lights, 2005), 238–241

The demand for justice is indeed a persistent part of the Jewish sources from the Bible to our own day, and it is a significant element in Jewish visions for the future.

This includes both procedural justice and substantive justice. Procedural justice demands that people be treated fairly in court and in society generally, with distinctions drawn among persons only for reasons having to do with their own actions or skills. So, for example, a just society is one in which people are not judged guilty or innocent, or fit for a job, according to the color of their skin or how much money they currently have.

2. Michael Lerner, "Election 2008: Why Is it Close?" *Tikkun* [Sept./Oct. 2008], 9

The simple reality is that many Americans are no more ready to let go of their racism than of their sexism or homophobia. The fear of Blacks is very deep in American culture and goes back many centuries. That fear is easy to understand: the recognition on the part of Whites that we as a society and a people have significantly contributed to the suffering of Blacks and never fully rectified the pain that we caused makes us scared that at any moment Black people will erupt with the anger that they justifiably might feel at this history of oppression and denial. This justifiable anger is not just based on historical memory; the reality is that Blacks continue to be the last hired, first fired in much of this country, that they are far more likely to be harassed for no reason other than their skin color, or arrested and jailed by police for crimes like drug possession that many Whites have committed without consequences.

3. Clergy statement, Jews for Marriage Equality. Available at http://www.jewsformarriageequality.org/DOWNLOADS/J4ME_Clergy_Statement_Aug_08_2008.pdf

We as rabbis, cantors and community leaders committed to Jewish tradition urge all Jews to remember our heritage of justice and to recommit ourselves to not wavering on this holy principle. We take heed of our historic mission to bring all Jews into the community and to bring peace to all persons. We join together as brothers and sisters in faith and call for an end to the shameful and hurtful idea that some families are less worthy and less human than others. All are created *b'tzelem elohim*, in the image of God. We acknowledge that gays and lesbians have too often been excluded, and we pledge to correct this inequality—both by fighting any and all legislative efforts to deprive gays and lesbians of their human and civil rights, including the right to marry—and by continuing to redouble our efforts to make every gay and lesbian family member, friend, colleague and congregant feel welcome in our synagogues and community as equals to their heterosexual neighbors.

4. Michael Medved, "Special 'Protections' For a Marginalized Majority?," May 27, 2009. Available at http://townhall.com/columnists/MichaelMedved/2009/05/27/special_protections_for_a_marginalized_majority

… race and sexual orientation are not comparable: even if homosexuality stems from innate urges that the individual can't control, the expression of those impulses (like all sexual behavior) involves elements of choice. The acceptance of gay marriage as the equivalent of traditional marriage will, however, make any such arguments moot. Once the government declares that there is no meaningful difference between the union of two men, two women, or a man and a woman, and affirms that banning gay marriage makes no more sense than banning interracial marriage … it embraces the idea that sexual minorities deserve legal protection in the same sense that racial minorities need it. For religious groups (whether representing minorities or, currently, majorities) the choice to maintain distinctions between same sex unions and traditional marriage—the choice to discriminate, in other words—will receive no such protection …

Hate Crimes

5. **Paul Goldenberg, Testimony at Hearing of United States Helsinki Commission, June 16, 2004. Available at http://www.ajc.org/site/apps/nlnet/content2.aspx?c=ioJNISOyErH&b=2690691&ct=3805519**

During my travels to other jurisdictions and nations, I have personally seen seasoned and jaded law enforcement officers who were disdainful of the impact of hate crime who, once well trained, not only understood the damage these crimes do to the fabric of social order, but became energized to find effective ways to combat them. They became motivated by a desire to protect and serve their citizenry, and facilitate the administration of justice for their nation.

From years of experience, North American law enforcement officials now understand a simple lesson: one hate crime in a community may seem inconsequential compared to other crimes, but they open the door to further incidents which can easily escalate into a larger order maintenance problem or public safety concern.

6. **Jeff Jacoby, "Punish Crime, Not Thought Crime" in *The Hate Debate: Should Hate Be Punished as a Crime?* Paul Iganski, ed. (London: Profile Books, 2002), 122**

Every offence covered by a hate crime law was illegal to begin with. Each one could have been prosecuted under existing criminal code. It may sound admirable to talk of 'preventing hate crimes' with new laws, but such laws prevent nothing except social unity. What they promote is balkanization, class warfare and identity politics.

Equal protection under the law is the ideal of every democratic society. A government that takes that ideal seriously tells potential criminals that they will be punished fully and fairly, regardless of the identity of their victims. Hate crime laws, by contrast, declare that some victims are more deserving than others. That is a message no citizen should be willing to accept.

7. **Anti-Defamation League, "Hate Crimes Laws." Available at http://www.adl.org/99hatecrime/penalty.asp**

The core of the ADL legal approach is a "penalty-enhancement" concept. In a landmark decision issued in June 1993, the United States Supreme Court unanimously upheld the constitutionality of Wisconsin's penalty-enhancement hate crimes statute, which was based on the ADL model. Expressions of hate protected by the First Amendment's free speech clause are not criminalized. However, criminal activity motivated by hate is subject to a stiffer sentence. A defendant's sentence may be enhanced if he intentionally selects his victim based upon his perception of the victim's race, religion, national origin, sexual orientation or gender.

Affirmative Action

8. **Albert Vorspan and David Saperstein, *Jewish Dimensions of Social Justice: Tough Moral Choices of Our Time* (New York: UAHC Press, 1998), 212–213**

At first glance, it would seem that reconciling affirmative action with Jewish tradition might prove difficult, as suggested by the following statement that says the rich and poor should not be treated differently by judges: "You shall do no unrighteousness in judgment; you shall not respect the person of the poor nor favor the person of the mighty, but in righteousness shall you judge your neighbor" (Leviticus 19:15). Yet even this clear position was bent to the realities of creating justice. In a well-known talmudic story about a dispute between brothers, the rules of evidence were changed to put an excessive burden on the rich and powerful brother when witnesses for the weaker brother were fearful of testifying. "Thus do we do for all who are powerful," says the text. (Babylonian Talmud, *Baba Metzia* 39b) The promise of equality is not sufficient if there are obstacles that make the reality of equality impossible.

9. **American Jewish Committee, statement on civil rights. Available at http://www.ajc.org/site/c.ijITI2PHKoG/b.838243/k.B0AB/Civil _Rights.htm**

AJC historically has supported a wide range of affirmative action measures designed to recruit, train and promote those who have been disadvantaged and discriminated against in the past. While AJC recognizes that specific problems in the implementation of affirmative action need to be rectified, affirmative action will remain necessary so long as discrimination continues to plague our society.

AJC rejects rigid quotas, but, as a temporary measure, supports flexible goals and timetables, and, where there has been a demonstrated pattern of discrimination, moderate, selectively applied preferences. Affirmative action should not mean hiring, promoting, or admitting unqualified persons for or to anything ...

Since our ideal remains a society free of racism and sexism, where every individual may realize his or her potential to the fullest based on merit, group rights must not prevail over individual rights. A thoughtful and well-balanced affirmative action policy is an important tool in achieving that idea.

10. Republican Jewish Coalition, Affirmative Action policy platform. Available at http://www.rjchq.org/About/policyplatformdetail.aspx? id=781ef803-eec8–4b89–9363–8ae5b21a5765

The cornerstone of a free society is equality of opportunity, not a government-mandated "equality" of result. All Americans, being equal citizens with equal rights under the law, have the right to be judged on their individual talents, skills, and achievements.

Affirmative action, goals, timetables, and set asides are often merely euphemisms for quotas. These devices violate the equal protection provisions of the 14th Amendment when implemented by state governments. When used by the federal government, private employers, colleges, and other entities, they violate the Civil Rights Act of 1964. Such quotas divide society, pitting group against group and race against race in an illegal search for proportional representation ...

The RJC categorically condemns racism and discrimination. It supports the full enforcement of all state and federal laws against discrimination. In keeping with the principle of equality under the law, the RJC opposes the use of quotas, goals, set-asides and other programs which give preferences to specific racial or ethnic groups, whether in regard to educational opportunities, business contracts, grants or loans, employment or other opportunities. They are ineffective, and ultimately harmful, policy tools.

11. Jonah Goldberg, "Racism by Any Other Name," *National Review* [Nov. 15, 2006]

It's time to admit that "diversity" is code for racism. If it makes you feel better, we can call it "nice" racism or "well-intentioned" racism or "racism that's good for you." Except that's the rub: It's racism that may be good for you if "you" are a diversity guru, a rich white liberal, a college administrator or one of sundry other types. But the question of whether diversity is good for "them" is a different question altogether, and much more difficult to answer.

... without racial preferences, Asians would take roughly 80 percent of the positions now allotted to Hispanic and black students.

In other words, there is a quota—though none dare call it that—keeping Asians out of elite schools in numbers disproportionate to their merit. This is the same sort of quota once used to keep Jews out of the Ivy League—not because of their lack of qualifications, but because having too many Jews would change the "feel" of, say, Harvard or Yale. Today, it's the same thing, only we've given that feeling a name: diversity.

12. Albert Vorspan and David Saperstein, *Jewish Dimensions of Social Justice: Tough Moral Choices of Our Time* (New York: UAHC Press, 1998), 213

Modern Israel has comfortably and systematically used affirmative action—even quotas—with great social effectiveness. In its early pioneering period, in the 1920s, the *Yishuv*—the nascent Jewish community in Palestine—invoked a doctrine known as *kibbush avodah*, the conquest of labor. Jewish landowners were importuned to hire Jewish workers to do manual labor. This was not because Jews were better at this type of work than their Arab neighbors; instead, it was because the leaders of the *Yishuv* understood that there needed to be a Jewish working class if there was to be a productive and successful Jewish society. Israel's legendary first prime minister, David Ben-Gurion, once told Leonard Fein, director of the Commission on Social Action of Reform Judaism, that in his opinion *kibbush avodah* was "the single most important element in preparing the way for a Jewish state." This is a compelling example of why, in some situations, society needs, at least temporarily, to base decisions on more than mere "merit" (i.e., the talents of candidates) alone.

Responses

For Whom is the Fight Against Discrimination?
Jews, Liberal Equality and Ethnic-Nationalism
Joseph Gindi

M ANY AMERICAN Jews grow up thinking that what it means to
be Jewish is to fight for equality and social justice. Jewish community leaders proudly talk about Jewish involvement in the Civil Rights
Movement, and young Jews are taught about the Jewish "tradition" of
tikkun olam (repair of the world). However, the American Jewish relationship to discrimination is no simple matter.

In this essay, I understand discrimination to mean the often institutionalized distinctions made between people based on pervasive social
hierarchies. The concept of discrimination itself makes sense only in
light of the Enlightenment ideal of citizenship. It is in the very process of
defining who is a citizen that a nation ascribes certain groups status as
"minorities," and thus must establish equality before the law in order to
ameliorate the disadvantages of that status.

In the course of partial European emancipation, two basic enduring
responses to minorities and the discrimination they faced developed.
These responses were both mutually dependent and in serious tension
with each other.[1] Enlightenment liberalism attempted to include minorities in the political body by creating a model of the abstract universal
citizen with whom the state could interact. Nationalism, on the other
hand, attempted to exclude minorities by demanding a relatively strict
correspondence between people, land, and state.[2]

Each of these responses has its limitations. Universal citizenship
has historically demanded homogeneity or assimilation, the erasure of
some elements of ethnic specificity. On the other hand, nationalism,

---

1. For the interdependency of nationalism and liberal citizenship see Aamir Mufti,
*Enlightenment in the Colony: The Jewish Question and the Crisis of Postcolonial
Culture* (Princeton, NJ: Princeton University Press, 2007).
2. While socialist internationalism can be identified as a third response to the Jewish
position in Europe, it never really took root in America, and is thus not included in
this essay.

47

particularly in its ethnic or religious variety, has tremendous difficulty absorbing minorities. The logic of nationalism, where the state exists to serve the interests of the nation rather than those of its citizens, leads toward the creation of exclusionary policies. Some minorities may be granted citizenship, but public policy then must ensure they maintain their minority status, or the national character of the state will be in jeopardy. Thus, we may say that liberalism incorporates, and then neutralizes difference, while nationalism excludes it.

By and large, mainstream American Jews came to embrace both of these basic approaches to discrimination with little recognition of their contradictions.[3] This essay will explore the history of this paradoxical embrace, a story of the pursuit of perceived Jewish interest in light of Jews' position as an assimilable minority within a liberal democracy.

Early Jewish-American Responses to Discrimination

The first significant wave of Jewish immigrants, mostly merchants from Central Europe who practiced Reform Judaism, arrived in the mid-19th century and quickly acculturated to America. Influenced by the Protestant theology of social gospel, the Reform Movement's 1885 statement of principles known as the Pittsburgh Platform declared that the mission of modern Judaism was, "to solve, on the basis of justice and righteousness, the problems presented by the contrasts and evils of the present organization of society."[4] As 20th-century scholar Arthur Hertzberg made clear, high-society Jewish reformers were not advocating for the restructuring of society, but for the amelioration of poverty and discrimination along liberal lines—goals more social than spiritual, and more American than uniquely Jewish.[5]

The relative ease of integration experienced by German Jews would later be challenged by the arrival of over two million Eastern European Jews from approximately 1880–1920.[6] These Jews entered an America that was increasingly consumed with the theories of scientific racism (eugenics, for

---

3. Throughout this essay, unless otherwise noted, the terms "the Jewish community" or even "American Jews" will usually refer to that constellation of organizations that claim to represent Jews in American social life and the individuals who share their perspective. I am using this terminology because it allows me to explore mainstream positions as such, not because I understand these to be the only, or the correct, Jewish positions.
4. Arthur Hertzberg, *The Jews in America: Four Centuries of an Uneasy Encounter* (New York: Simon and Schuster, 1989), 148.
5. Ibid.
6. Ibid., 152.

example) and a growing attitude of nativism. The racial logic of the time separated those we might now call white ethnics (for example, Jews, Italians, and Poles) into distinct racial categories such as Asiatics, Mediterraneans, Slavs, and others, all of whom occupied a position beneath that of the pure Anglo-Saxon.[7]

Large numbers of Eastern European immigrants, rapidly proletarianized in the American industrial economy, turned to the labor and socialist movements to combat their own exploitation and that of the working class more generally. These radical movements often rejected integrationist (democratic capitalist) and nationalist (Zionist) approaches in favor of a radically transformed relationship between workers, capital, and the state.[8] Yet, many others embraced capitalism and strove to become American, dropping their distinctive names and seeking to homogenize their appearance as they climbed the socioeconomic ladder.[9]

Despite the political, economic, and religious diversity of American Jews in the early 20th century, that period also witnessed the beginning of an organized American Jewish response to discrimination—domestically and internationally. Jews founded a number of organizations, including the American Jewish Committee (AJC), the Anti-Defamation League (ADL), and the American Jewish Congress (AJCongress), to encourage American diplomatic efforts to stop anti-Semitic pogroms in Europe, prevent the restriction of Eastern European immigration, combat acts of racial violence in America, and advocate for Zionism on the world stage. Although they differed on particulars, these organizations shared "the goal of linking Jews and their political interests with core American values and practices," putting the pursuit of Jewish security and Jewish interests in terms acceptable to American political culture.[10]

---

7. For Eastern European Jews' place in the American racial schema, see Matthew Frye Jacobson, *Whiteness of a Different Color: European Immigrants and the Alchemy of Race* (Cambridge, MA: Harvard University Press, 1998).

8. For a wonderful overview of American Jewish socialism, see Tony Michels, *A Fire in Their Hearts: Yiddish Socialists in New York* (Cambridge, MA: Harvard University Press, 2005).

9. See Riv-Ellen Prell, *Fighting to Become Americans: Assimilation and the Trouble between Jewish Women and Jewish Men* (Boston, MA: Beacon Press, 1999) for immigrant class anxiety and its relationship to gender.

10. Steven Windmueller, "Defenders: National Jewish Community Relations Agencies," in *Jewish Policy and American Civil Society: Communal Agencies and Religious Movements in the American Public Sphere,* Alan Mittleman, Robert A. Licht, and Jonathan D. Sarna, eds. (Lanham, MD: Rowman & Littlefield, 2002), 15.

The establishment and subsequent coordination of the AJC, ADL, and AJCongress helped to define what could be constituted as "Jewish" issues: fighting anti-Semitism and advocating for American support of Zionism and, later, of Israel.[11] Although many American Jews were certainly committed to liberal ideals, the strong stance taken by these organizations in the legal fight against discrimination, the promotion of interethnic and interreligious relations, and the defense of separation of church and state, represented an outgrowth of their primary mission to protect Jews.

Yet, even Zionism was not always central to communal politics. Cognizant of their tenuous place in American society, Jewish organizations in the early 20th century practiced an integrationist politics that historian Marc Dollinger has called a "politics of acculturation."[12] Deeply committed to this approach and fearful of the charge of double loyalty, the American Jewish Committee provided humanitarian support for Jews living in Palestine, but staunchly refused to support the Zionist political cause.[13] After the establishment of the State of Israel, the American Jewish Committee and the Anti-Defamation League moved toward the position of the American Jewish Congress in their twin embrace of Zionism and American liberalism. This led to the development of fundamental tensions between these agencies' embrace of liberal equality and their support for Zionism.

Jews and the Civil Rights Movement

Jewish communal policy began to divide at precisely the time that Jewish organizations were embarking on an alliance with Black civil rights organizations to push for racial equality.[14] This strong investment in the civil rights agenda masked the growing inconsistencies in Jewish communal policy regarding minorities and discrimination. Although Jewish communal leaders often invoke images of Jewish participation in the Civil Rights Movement as a testament to the fundamental Jewish opposition to discrimination, the reality is more complicated.

---

11. Ibid., 43–46.
12. Marc Dollinger, *Quest for Inclusion: Jews and Liberalism in Modern America* (Princeton, NJ: Princeton University Press, 2000), 80.
13. Ibid., 58.
14. In talking about Blacks and Jews, I do not wish to obscure the existence of Jews of color. I am rather focusing on the positioning of institutions and broader communities we can label Black and Jewish.

Many contemporary historians explain Jewish participation in the Civil Rights Movement as a reflection of a momentary convergence of interests and approaches, rather than an enduring Jewish commitment to justice.[15] As noted above, institutional Jewish responses to discrimination began as a way to protect Jews in America and abroad against discrimination. Yet, after World War II, a joint program brought Blacks and Jews together to combat anti-Semitism and racism. Jewish communal leaders began to see the fight against discrimination as a shared project, and recognized, in the wake of the Holocaust, that hatred and discrimination anywhere and of any kind were not good for the Jews, and that anti-Semitism could be addressed through intergroup cooperation. Black and Jewish communal leaders and organizations worked together for desegregation, the abolition of restrictive housing covenants, and the elimination of quotas and discriminatory admissions policies at colleges and universities.[16]

Although the alliance held as the Civil Rights Movement transformed into a popular movement agitating for voting rights and integration, it began to unravel in the wake of its partial success. The liberal approach to civil rights allowed for some of the most blatant discrimination to be struck down, helping Jews achieve greater economic success and relatively seamless integration into American society. For many of them, this led to an expectation that other minorities would follow the same path. Yet, many Blacks were left to struggle with staggering social and economic hurdles. This reality caused increasing tensions between Jews and Blacks, as Blacks sought more radical approaches to ameliorate their condition, including an embrace of Black Nationalism.

Such tensions produced a reassessment of which alliances served Jewish self-interest. As a result, many Jewish organizations abandoned their attempts to address deep structural inequalities that continued to adversely affect Blacks. Major Black and Jewish organizations thus took opposing stances on the affirmative action cases of the 1970s.[17] This shift in perceived self-interest was coupled with the simultaneous embrace of divergent nationalisms. Zionism only intensified as Jewish fear and pride

---

15. See Dollinger, *Quest for Inclusion*, and Cheryl Lynn Greenberg, *Troubling the Waters: Black-Jewish Relations in the American Century* (Princeton, NJ: Princeton University Press, 2006), for a discussion of the relationship of Jewish interests to liberalism in the civil rights period.
16. Greenberg, 9–11.
17. Ibid., 239.

surged in the wake of the Six-Day War, while the Black Nationalist movement embraced support for Palestinians living under Israeli occupation. It became clear that, at home and abroad, Jewish and Black organizations no longer shared the same agenda.[18]

It is at this point in history when the contradictions in mainstream Jewish approaches to discrimination began to reveal themselves. American Jewish organizations opposed affirmative action for Blacks, fearful that it would cut into Jewish socioeconomic gains. However, they supported affirmative action for Jews on the world stage in the form of the State of Israel, whose existence was based largely on the premise that in light of historical injustices, some people deserved preferential treatment in the global political arena. Ironically, while many Jews were alienated by Black Nationalism, the very success of Jewish integration and increasing Jewish comfort in America enabled American Jews to eschew their "politics of acculturation" and embrace their own nationalism without fear of being charged with double loyalty. The shock of the Holocaust and the establishment of the State of Israel in 1948 have in fact turned Zionism into a central tenet of the organized Jewish community.

Contradictions and Tensions

The organized Jewish community now embraces a fully bifurcated political philosophy. On domestic matters, mainstream Jewish organizations trumpet opposition to discrimination, support for equal protection under the law, and defense of the separation of church and state. On international matters, they generally work to promote Israel's interests and seek to protect Israel's status as an explicitly Jewish state.

Tension between these positions on domestic and international issues has only increased in recent years. In their Israeli policy, however, few mainstream organizations have invested significant resources to work

18. For the turn toward Black nationalism and its relationship to Third World nationalism, see William L. Van Deburg, *Modern Black Nationalism: From Marcus Garvey to Louis Farrakhan* (New York: New York University Press, 1997). For the radical Jewish embrace of Zionism and its relationship to Black nationalism, see Jack Nusan Porter and Peter Dreier, *Jewish Radicalism: A Selected Anthology* (New York: Grove Press, 1973) and Michael Staub, *Torn at the Roots: The Crisis of Jewish Liberalism in Postwar America* (New York: Columbia University Press, 2002). For the impact of the Six-Day War on American Jews, see Eli Lederhendler, *The Six-Day War and World Jewry* (Bethesda, MD: University Press of Maryland, 2000).

toward the separation of church and state in Israel or the establishment of equal protection for non-Jews. The most glaring contradiction between these goals and current American Jewish communal policy is, of course, that organizations who claim to support equality and democracy refuse to speak out strongly against Israel's occupation of territories that include over three million Palestinians or to advocate for Israel to be a state for all its citizens. It has gotten to the point where once stalwart defenders of civil rights are now fomenting intense fear and anti-Arab racism in order to ensure American support of Israeli policy. This attenuation of public commitment to equality and civil rights has led to a shift in the makeup of the dominant Jewish communal organizations.

For my generation of activists, the Anti-Defamation League and the American Jewish Congress are no longer seen as obvious organizations in which to invest time, energy, and resources in the pursuit of social justice, leaving those with more parochial concerns to fill the ranks of those agencies. Some activists concerned with advancing civil rights, fair immigration policy, or economic justice gravitate toward non-sectarian organizations. Others have flocked to a parallel universe of smaller, more focused Jewish organizations, which more pointedly proclaim themselves as advocates for social justice and have generally avoided the appearance of hypocrisy that many young activists identify with the politics of the old guard.[19]

As a matter of both focus and prudence, some of these smaller organizations define their missions narrowly enough to avoid dealing with the question of Zionism. Unfortunately, these organizations recognize that in order to maintain their clout within the world of organized Jewry, they often need to abandon or play down a commitment to pursuing equality and justice with regard to Israel or the Israeli/Palestinian conflict. Other organizations feel they cannot abandon their commitment to equality even when it comes to Israel and have chosen to advocate for an end to the occupation of Palestinian territories as they advocate for issues such as immigration and the death penalty.

---

19. These organizations range from those with a national agenda like Jewish Funds for Justice or American Jewish World Service to those with a local focus like the Progressive Jewish Alliance in Los Angeles and San Francisco, the Jewish Council on Urban Affairs in Chicago, and Jews United for Justice in Washington, DC. For profiles of some of the latter, see Melanie Kaye/Kantrowitz, *The Colors of Jews: Racial Politics and Radical Diasporism* (Bloomington, IN: Indiana University Press, 2007).

The Way Forward

The expansion of this universe of smaller organizations with explicit social justice missions offers one possible path through the struggle between liberalism and nationalism. As America moves beyond identity politics, these new organizations embrace a commitment to equality through the nurturing of difference. Such organizations as Rabbis for Human Rights and Peace Now generally demand that the basic liberal tenet of equality be pursued in Israel, as well.

I see all of these developments as positive. For instance, activist April Rosenblum's masterful work demonstrates that the fight against anti-Semitism, the foundational aim of the traditional "defense" organizations, can be conducted as part of a larger commitment to anti-racist and anti-imperialist solidarity.[20] As a new generation of Jewish activists pursues justice *lishmah*, "for its own sake," I hope that the Jewish community can turn from asking, "What is good for the Jews?" to asking, "What is good for all of us, including Jews?" I am also hopeful that a new generation of activists committed to political involvement in the Diaspora will no longer consider the State of Israel an exception to their agenda and will demand that Israel extend basic rights of equal protection to all people under its control.

The Jewish fight against discrimination is most powerful when it is part of broader movements for social change, and when it is taken up by diverse coalitions pursing policies that simultaneously further the general good and their particular interests. Jews are most effective and morally justified in this fight when they apply the same demands for equality to societies where they are the minority as they do to societies where they are the majority—battling discrimination even, or especially, when the perpetrators are Jews. Finally, this fight is also strengthened when Jews work to combat discrimination as *Jews*, powerfully reaffirming their minority identity, which makes them both a threatened and protected group within the liberal state.

---

20. To download a copy of April Rosenblum's activist handbook on resisting anti-Semitism, go to http://pinteleyid.com/past/. An excerpted version can be found in *Righteous Indignation: A Jewish Call for Justice,* Or N. Rose, Jo Ellen Green Kaiser, and Margie Klein, eds. (Woodstock, VT: Jewish Lights, 2008).

Discrimination: A Violation of Human Dignity
Rachel Kahn-Troster

"All human beings are born free and equal in dignity and rights. They are endowed with reason and conscience and should act towards one another in a spirit of brotherhood." (Article 1, Universal Declaration of Human Rights, United Nations, 1948)

ONE PIECE of Torah that I often turn to is the Universal Declaration of Human Rights (UDHR), proclaimed by a fledgling United Nations in December 1948. Written as a reaction to the Holocaust and the other atrocities of World War II, in a time of profound human brokenness, its preamble begins: "Whereas recognition of the inherent dignity and of the equal and inalienable rights of all members of the human family is the foundation of freedom, justice and peace in the world … " I think this is a deeply Jewish text, as it asserts that every single person inherently has dignity and is entitled to respect. Such a view reflects the rabbinic value of *kavod ha-beriyot*, respect for the dignity of all creation, which serves as the core Jewish ideal of human relationships. As a Jew and as a citizen, I am inspired by the Declaration's objective of achieving "freedom, justice, and peace" based on the recognition of human dignity, and so I strive to think of the dignity of others in my daily interactions. Practice *kavod ha-beriyot*, the Declaration tells us, and you can bring about *tikkun olam*, the repair of the world.

Article 2 of the UDHR states: "Everyone is entitled to all the rights and freedoms set forth in this Declaration, without distinction of any kind, such as race, color, sex, language, religion, political or other opinion, national or social origin, property, birth or other status." Therefore, the end of discrimination is an international goal for our world, not just a lofty American concern. Under international law, no one is more or less of a person. Discrimination, both legal and social, is the antithesis of *kavod ha-beriyot* because it begins with making distinctions between people, thus denying the shared humanity of all people.

I've heard others claim that discrimination is human, that we are hardwired to want to hold onto our own competitive advantage over those who are different from, or perhaps not related to, us. I believe that Judaism wants us to reach beyond this less holy impulse. The Talmud (Berakhot 19b) taught that a concern for *kavod ha-beriyot* overrides rabbinic prohibitions—a bold statement. This is because laws are worth nothing if we use them to deny our shared humanity with others.

Discrimination's Impact on My Family

I feel strongly about the dangers of discrimination because I'm keenly aware of the effects of social and legal discrimination. I've seen them in my own family. In 1930s Toronto, my paternal grandfather was the first member of his family to go to a university. He received a degree in chemical engineering, but he couldn't find work in his field because he was Jewish. Instead, he went to work in the family shoe factory, and then enlisted in the Canadian Army during World War II. By the time he returned, Jews were able to get work in chemical engineering, but the war had vastly changed the field, and now it was too late for him. With a family to support, my grandfather had to leave a career in the sciences to the next generation.

In 1930s Germany, my maternal grandfather was the last boy to have a bar mitzvah in his synagogue before it was destroyed on Kristallnacht, the "Night of Broken Glass," a pogrom in which thousands of Jewish synagogues, businesses, and homes across that country were damaged or destroyed. My great-grandmother managed to get her immediate family to Canada before it was too late, but they had already experienced some of the terrible legal discrimination that the German Jewish community suffered under the Nazis, instituted under the Nuremberg Laws. My grandfather rarely spoke about what had happened during that time, but it was clear what forces were responsible for uprooting the family. Laws can be used to codify social discrimination, which, in turn, can be the harbinger of far worse things. Thus, my family history has driven me to react strongly to concerns about both social and legal discrimination.

I often feel that people who claim that there are legitimate reasons for certain forms of discrimination are merely rationalizing policies that are not truly necessary. Many of the reasons for legal discrimination seem more like excuses for people's prejudices. For instance, in a country that has always been a haven for immigrants, why do we pursue legislation that punishes illegal immigrants or that tightens immigration restrictions? Why can't someone born abroad become the president of the United States if he or she becomes a U.S. citizen? The purpose of the law should be to protect minorities, not to exclude them based on rationales for national policy that are often motivated by personal prejudice.

I acknowledge that the concept of equal protection under the law can be a matter of perspective. For example, I'm a mother, and I depend on laws that ensure my right to breastfeed in public and take maternity leave without fear of losing my job. However, does my right to take maternity leave result in discrimination against my co-workers without children who might have to cover for me while I am out? How do we balance the needs of disparate constituencies? And if we truly treated each other from a place of *kavod ha-beriyot*, would we even need laws to guarantee equal protection of various groups? Maybe the laws that prevent discrimination can be more accurately framed as laws that help each and every one of us get what we need to fulfill our potential. But that's a fluid and flexible goal, and hard to legislate.

Discrimination and the Law

Systemic discrimination, such as institutionalized racism, is very far from being abolished in the United States. However, this type of discrimination can be subtle, leaving us each to wonder how we know when we are being discriminated against. Thus, when I experience what I perceive to be sexism or ageism on the job, I often second-guess my intuition, trying to find an alternate explanation. This hesitation is why attempts by the courts to limit the right to sue for workplace discrimination are so damaging.

It might take years of working for a company before a woman even realizes she is unfairly being paid less than a male counterpart for the same position and duties. It might take even longer for her to recognize less clear-cut forms of discrimination, such as being given less work because she either has children or might have them in the future, or being unaware of important information because her male colleagues exclude her from socializing. Such unequal treatment may be grounds for a gender discrimination lawsuit, but the less concrete the discrimination, the harder it is to prove, and the trickier it is to legislate. Laws limiting the right to sue for workplace discrimination only increase a woman's hesitation to pursue gender discrimination lawsuits, and makes a case for discrimination much more challenging if a woman does decide to sue.

Discrimination and Same-Sex Marriage

The debate over same-sex marriage raises both the issue of legal discrimination and that of more subtle social discrimination. Discrimination against

57

people who are lesbian, gay, bisexual, or transgender (LGBT) seems to be one of the last commonly practiced forms of discrimination, in part because many people still believe that being gay is a "choice." Those who hold that belief feel that gay people shouldn't be legally protected from discrimination, because they could just make the discrimination go away by choosing to be straight. Similarly, they believe that many who are transgender could avoid discrimination by choosing to maintain the gender identity they were born with.

Largely because of such beliefs, not only are legal protections for homosexuals often defeated in elections, but also there is no national protection from discrimination on the basis of gender identity, and in many states, gay people are prohibited from adopting or fostering children. The battle over legalizing gay marriages, however, has had mixed results. Some states have voted to ban the practice, while others have passed legislation to legalize it. Opponents of gay marriage express the concern that same-sex unions will destroy the institution of heterosexual marriage. As such, they feel that discrimination in the form of outlawing gay marriage is necessary. But this is a rationalization, obscuring the central question of why the government has any business promoting heterosexual marriage at all. Why is a family springing from a heterosexual married couple valued over other forms of family units? Why can't everyone who wishes to be partnered get married? Opponents of gay marriage don't talk about these issues, instead cloaking themselves in victimhood, claiming their values are under attack. Yet, our society privileges heterosexual marriage in its laws, its visual images, and its values.

Discrimination and Privilege

In the debate over same-sex marriage, many of us are privileged. Most of us in opposite-sex marriages don't think about the many rights we automatically obtain when we marry, including the rights to inherit from and to make health care decisions about our spouses. We can rely on having access to our loved ones in times of distress and can count on the equation of joint property rights with marriage. Those of us in heterosexual marriages don't have to think about these rights because no one will ever question them. When I married and had children, I became more aware of the less obvious forms of straight privilege that I enjoy. And that's part of the problem: when we only focus on ending discrimination and fail to examine our own privilege, we continue to participate in a discriminatory system.

I am reminded of ways in which, when women were first granted more equal employment opportunities, they were expected to conform to rules of workplace behavior created by men. The women who entered these workplaces needed to learn to mimic their privileged male colleagues without actually being part of that privileged group, while their own knowledge and experience may not have been equally valued. Equal opportunity is, therefore, not enough (though it would make a big difference in helping us each scrutinize the degree to which privilege affects our lives). I have to be willing to cede some of the power my privilege provides me and more closely examine who is put at a disadvantage because of my privilege.

Yet, it is easier to claim discrimination than to understand privilege. I once read a wonderful essay describing 50 things white Americans take for granted that black Americans do not, including seeing families similar to theirs in the media (and portrayed positively), and not being constantly defined as a spokesperson for their entire group or having their behavior understood as a representation of that entire group. Though most Jews are now considered to be white, many can probably relate to such feelings of exclusion and the problem of being viewed as a representative for their entire minority group. But many Jews can also acknowledge that they benefit from white privilege. For instance, I stopped watching one cable channel because I never saw anyone on it who looked like me or anyone else in my New York neighborhood—no Jews, very few people of color, no one with an accent. I felt excluded by the media in this case, and noted the exclusion of others. Despite that, I am certain that no cop would ever stop my car because of the color of my skin. This is just one way in which I reap the benefits of white privilege.

Social Discrimination: Treatment of the Overweight

More pervasive than discrimination and privilege based on categories of race, gender, or sexual orientation, is social discrimination based on appearance. In fact, many of the most pervasive stereotypes in our society are of fat people. They are often portrayed as lazy, slovenly, and unable to control themselves. Studies have shown that people who are overweight are discriminated against in hiring and promotions (though with an interesting gender twist: this affects women more than men). As with arguments against same-sex marriage and legal protections for homosexuals, the language of choice is applied to the overweight. Some argue that people choose to overeat and become fat, and that they could choose to become thin again—whether or not this corresponds with reality. The failure to make the choice to "be thin" is regarded by many as a moral failing, and is seen as legitimizing ridicule. Being thin is considered a virtue, a sign of self-control and a result of healthy choices.

This moral equation denies that there are healthy people who are overweight, that there are often genetic causes for weight issues, or that we live in a country where government subsidies often result in making unhealthy food cheaper. Weight bias can be linked to class discrimination as well, as those who have access to organic groceries and the income to afford such groceries bemoan the "choices" made by those who lack access to organic foods and can only afford fast food.

No matter the cause of someone's obesity, weight is not the defining characteristic of his or her identity, and it shouldn't make him or her vulnerable to public criticism and ridicule. Social discrimination against the overweight is much more open than other types of discrimination. Many people would never comment about someone's race (at least not openly), but feel free to criticize another's weight. Biases against those who are overweight thus more easily manifest into discrimination in the workplace and in other social settings.

The Jewish Response to Discrimination

I don't think classical Jewish sources ever confronted a problem like the modern issue of discrimination, but that doesn't mean that Jewish values don't inform my own ideal of a just society. That society is one that does not allow for discrimination. The following midrash from *Genesis Rabbah* 24 serves as one of the foundations for the idea of *kavod ha-beriyot*:

> Ben Azzai says: 'This is the record of Adam's line' (Gen. 5:1) is the foremost principle in the Torah. R. Akiva says: 'Love your neighbor as yourself' (Lev. 19:18), this is the greatest principle of the Torah. You should not say: Because I have been dishonored, let my fellow man be dishonored along with me ... R. Tanhuma explained: If you do so, know whom you are dishonoring—'God made him in the likeness of God' (Gen. 5:1).

The Rabbis in this midrash do not disagree that humans have an obligation to each other. What is in question here is why we have that obligation. Is it because we have shared parentage, all descending from Adam and Eve? Is it because we must treat each other as we hope to be treated?

Or is it because dishonoring another person dishonors God, as we are all created in God's image?

In this midrash, *kavod ha-beriyot*, respect for human dignity, becomes the foremost principle of the Torah, meaning that all people have an obligation to treat each other with respect. Neglecting these values enables us to convince ourselves, consciously or unconsciously, that some people are less deserving than others of equal protection under the law and of being treated with common decency. As Jews, *kavod ha-beriyot* can't just be a textual value, left to some rabbis to debate on a forgotten page. It must be a lived value.

I am sure that many of us know the pain of being seen through the lens of a stereotype, and of being told that it would be better if we developed a thicker skin when we get offended by those stereotypes. But I don't think God envisioned human beings creating a world where we cause each other such pain. However, although those of us involved in Jewish social justice work often invoke the principle of *tikkun olam*, which means repairing or perfecting the world, we don't often say what we hope a better world will look like. For me, it is a given that we must work toward a world like the one envisioned so eloquently in the Universal Declaration of Human Rights— one in which the dignity and equality of every person is recognized.

If we each live a life guided by *kavod ha-beriyot*, we will help repair the world.

Bias Crime Laws and the Mission of Social Justice
Frederick M. Lawrence

B IAS CRIMES are a scourge on our society. Is there a more terrifying image in the mind's eye than that of the burning cross? Crimes that are motivated by prejudice make a uniquely compelling call on our conscience. Legislators have often reacted to them with remarkable alacrity. When predominantly Black churches were in flames across the South during the summer of 1996, it took only a matter of weeks for Congress to enact and for President Clinton to sign the Church Arson Prevention Act.

The case study here asks whether the perpetrators of bias crimes should be charged with special circumstances in addition to their primary crime, or what I have called the "parallel crime," such as assault or homicide. It also asks whether being a racist murderer instead of "just" a murderer should affect one's sentence. I answer this question strongly in the affirmative.

The question of punishment for bias crimes involves two significant sets of issues, one dealing with the philosophical and legal bases for criminal punishment and sentencing, and the other dealing with matters of free expression. This essay argues that enhancing punishments for bias crimes is not only permitted by doctrines of criminal law and free expression, but is actually mandated by our societal commitment to the ideal of equality.

The Nature of Bias Crimes
It is best to begin with a brief discussion of precisely what a bias crime is. I prefer the term "bias crime" to the more popularly used term "hate crime." Although "hate crime" is a powerfully evocative term, "bias crime" captures more precisely what is at stake when we analyze violent and criminal manifestations of prejudice.

The essential element of a bias-motivated crime is that the perpetrator commits the offense because of the victim's race, ethnicity, religion, national origin, sexual orientation, or other group identification. Many instances of personal, violent crimes may be motivated all or in part by hatred per se for the victim. If, however, there were no bias motivation, this conduct would not be considered a civil rights crime. Bias is thus best understood as a special case of hatred, one based on group membership and expressing a form of discrimination that has a social and historical context. However evocative the phrase "hate crime" may be, it can distract from and obscure what is really at stake, whereas the term "bias crime" focuses and clarifies that.

What, then, is a bias crime? While the answer looks both to the motivation of the criminal and the results of his or her conduct, the motivation—what is known in criminal law doctrine as *mens rea*—is the key to identifying a bias crime. For example, Colin Ferguson's December 1993 shooting spree on the Long Island Rail Road—carefully directed only at white and Asian-American passengers—was a bias crime. In contrast, an interracial fight between a landlord and tenant that erupts following an argument over the level of heat provided to the tenant is not a bias crime.

So, which biases constitute a "bias motivation?" Who is a victim of a bias crime?

The answers have their roots in a society's very definition of itself. "Bias" should include bigotry on the basis of race, ethnicity, religion, national origin, sexual orientation, and in certain instances, gender. A particular bias crime statute may include additional characteristics. Indeed, the scope of what constitutes "bias" adopted by a particular legislature is a significant statement of that society's values and its sense of equality. This essay assumes that, for the purposes of this case study, the legislature has settled upon the categories that are to be included in a bias crime statute.

Determining what a bias crime is and the categories of its victims leaves two critical questions for consideration: whether bias crimes deserve enhanced punishment, and whether enhanced punishment of bias crimes is an inappropriate punishment of "thought crime" or is consonant with principles of free expression.

The Enhanced Punishment of Bias Crimes

Crimes consist of two elements: criminal intent, or *mens rea*, and the criminal act, or *actus reus*. Similarly, the severity of a crime is determined by two factors: the *mens rea* of the actor and the harm his or her act causes. Determining the severity of a crime is critical in the process of determining the appropriate sentence to be imposed. Proportionality is a key concept in criminal punishment, whether we believe as did Immanuel Kant and other retributivists that punishment is based on what the perpetrator deserves for the crime committed, or whether we instead agree with Jeremy Bentham and other utilitarians that punishment is based on

63

achieving the optimal deterrence of crime for the greatest good to society. The requirement that "the punishment fit the crime" reflects that sense of proportionality, so in order to determine the relative punishments for various crimes, there must be a means by which to measure the relative seriousness of those crimes.

Where the level of intentionality for two crimes is roughly the same— as is often the case with assault and murder—the relative seriousness of the crimes is best measured by the harm caused: murder is worse than even the most purposeful assault. Similarly, when comparing intentional assaults and intentional bias-motivated assaults, we would look to the harm caused by each category of crime to determine suitable punishment. Although we cannot measure relative harm with arithmetic precision, numerous factors can guide our understanding: the nature of the injury sustained by the immediate victim of a bias crime; the palpable harm inflicted on the target community; and the harm to society at large. When we apply this analysis of relative harm to bias crimes, we see that bias crimes warrant harsher punishment than "parallel crimes," similar crimes lacking bias motivation.

A bias criminal attacks the victim not only physically, but at the very core of his or her identity, making it an attack from which there is no escape. It is one thing to avoid the park at night because it is not safe. It is quite another to avoid certain neighborhoods because of one's race or religion, for example. This heightened sense of vulnerability caused by bias crimes is beyond that normally found in crime victims. The victims of bias crimes tend to experience psychological symptoms such as depression, withdrawal, anxiety, feelings of helplessness, and a profound sense of isolation. Additionally, bias-motivated attacks, when directed against minority victims, trigger the history and social context of prejudice and hate-motivated violence against the victim and the victim's group. Hence, the bias component of crimes committed against minority group members is not merely associated with prejudice per se, but usually with prejudice against a member of a historically oppressed group.

The impact of bias crimes reaches beyond the harm done to the immediate victim or victims of the criminal behavior. There is a more widespread impact on the "target community"—that is, the community that shares the race, religion, or ethnicity of the victim—and an even broader harm to society in general. Members of a target community experience a bias crime far more deeply than the public experiences a parallel crime.

64

The reaction of the target community is one of empathy with the victim, and members of that community often perceive the crime as if they were each directly attacked.

Consider the burning of a cross on the lawn of an African-American family or the spray-painting of swastikas and hateful graffiti on the home of a Jewish family. Others might associate themselves with the injuries done to these families, have feelings of anger or hurt, and sympathize with the victims. The reactions of members of the target community, however, will transcend those. The cross-burning and the swastika-scrawling will conjure more than similar feelings of victimhood and fear on the part of other Blacks and Jews respectively. Rather, members of these target communities may experience further threats and attacks stemming from these initial crimes. The additional harm of real or perceived personal threats to people other than the immediate victims differentiates a bias crime from a parallel crime and makes it more harmful to society.

Finally, the impact of bias crimes may spread well beyond the immediate victims and the target community to the general society. This effect encompasses a large array of harms from the very concrete to the most abstract. On the most mundane level—but by no means the least damaging—the resulting isolation of a particular group, as discussed above, has a cumulative effect on the community at large. Consider a family victimized by an act of bias-motivated vandalism who then begins to withdraw from society; the family members seek safety from an unknown assailant who, having sought them out for clear reasons, might do so again. Members of the community, even those who are sympathetic to the plight of the victim's family and who have been supportive of them, may be reluctant to place themselves in harm's way and may shy away from socializing with these victims or from letting their children do so. Thus, the isolation of this family will not be solely a result of their own withdrawal, but the community will isolate them as well, injuring both the family and society at large.

Bias crimes cause even broader injury to the general community by threatening the community's core values. Such crimes violate not only society's general concern for the security of its members and their property, but also the shared values of equality and racial and religious harmony in a heterogeneous society. A bias crime is therefore a profound violation of the egalitarian ideal and the opposition to discrimination that have become fundamental aspects of the American legal system, and of American culture as well.

This harm is, of course, highly contextual. We could imagine a society in which, for example, racial motivation for a crime would have no greater impact than the motivation of a perpetrator's dislike of their victim. Given America's legal and social history, however, ours is not such a society. Bias crimes implicate a social history of prejudice, discrimination, and even oppression. As such, they cause a greater harm than parallel crimes do to the immediate victim, the target community, and society at large.

The bias-motivated criminal seeks to inflict a greater harm than that caused by a crime of otherwise similar intensity with no bias motivation. The appropriate response of the criminal justice system is to identify the bias crime as something related to, but ultimately distinct from and worse than, the parallel crime, and to impose a criminal sentence of greater severity as a means of punishment.

The Conflict between the Punishment of Hate Crimes and Freedom of Expression

Although the question of whether bias criminals deserve enhanced punishment is significant, legal scholars, journalists, and other commentators have focused more attention on whether the enhanced punishment of bias criminals comports with our commitment to freedom of belief and expression. I refer to this as the "bias crimes/hate speech paradox." Is it possible to enhance the sentences for bias-motivated crimes when the right to free expression of ideas, no matter how distasteful or hateful, is a fundamental constitutional principle? How much intolerance a liberal democracy should tolerate is a question that has fueled debate for years.

The apparent paradox of seeking to punish the perpetrators of bias-motivated violence while being committed to protecting bigots' rights to express their prejudices is actually not a paradox at all. We must focus on the basic distinction between bias crimes and "hate speech": the criminal manifestation of prejudice may be punished, whereas the articulation of prejudicial views, no matter how unpleasant, is protected. This distinction has been blurred (or denied) by commentators and courts alike, including, for example, the Supreme Court in *R.A.V. v. City of St. Paul* (1992), in which the St. Paul, Minnesota ordinance banning cross-burning or other displays that "arouse anger, alarm or resentment in others on the basis of race, color, creed, religion or gender" was struck down; and in *Wisconsin v. Mitchell* (1993), in which the Wisconsin law providing enhanced penalties for bias-motivated crimes was upheld. Others have suggested either that both bias crimes and hate speech be protected, or that both be punished. But we may, and should, reject these extremes in favor of a middle position.

The basic distinction between a bias crime and hate speech lies in the underlying motivation of the actor, which can be ascertained by looking at the non-bias element of the behavior involved. The non-bias element of hate speech is expression, a form of behavior that, however offensive, is protected and should not be made criminal. Speech advocating racial superiority is, bias aside, the expression of an opinion. The non-bias element of a bias crime, however, is an actual parallel crime that is punishable. Burning a cross on the lawn of a Black family, bias aside, is still at least trespassing and would probably warrant a charge of endangerment, assault, or arson.

Free expression protects the right to express offensive views but not the right to behave criminally. This is true even when the parallel crime consists solely of speech. Bias-targeted behavior that is intended to create fear in its targeted victim or to incite others to bias-motivated violence is a bias crime. Behavior that vents the actor's bigotry and perhaps upsets the addressee greatly is, on the other hand, hate speech that is protected by the First Amendment. The enhanced punishment of bias crimes, therefore, is fully consonant with our constitutional guarantees of free expression.

The Broader Framework through Which to View Bias Crimes

Because racial harmony and equality are among the highest values held in our society, crimes that violate these values should be punished more harshly than crimes that, although otherwise similar, do not violate these values. Therefore, if bias crimes are not punished more harshly than parallel crimes, the message expressed by the criminal justice system is that racial harmony and equality are, in fact, not among our highest values. Put differently, it is impossible for the system of punishment a society sets up *not* to express that society's values. Our criminal justice system's treatment of bias crimes, therefore—specifically the identification of bias-motivated crimes as a particular category of crimes (or not) and the enhanced punishment of bias-motivated crimes (or not)—necessarily demonstrates the extent of our society's commitment to equality and its defense of difference. The punishment of bias crimes is therefore necessary for the full expression of a commitment to American values.

CASE 3

❧

THE ENVIRONMENT

Case Study

The Environment

1. Individual responsibility

Many people view their attempts to recycle and reduce their consumption of resources as noble acts of caring for the environment. Yet, some are skeptical as to whether their small, individual actions make a difference. How do we determine whether such acts are really making an environmental impact? Should one feel responsible for helping to protect the environment, and if so, how does one fulfill that responsibility? Should one's buying practices be affected by environmental considerations? Do individuals have a moral duty to reduce, reuse, and recycle? If so, why? If not, why not?

2. Corporate responsibility

The Widget Factory has been in business for 50 years, employing thousands of people and making a significant profit for its investors over time. In manufacturing its product, however, carbon dioxide and nitrogen are released into the atmosphere, and some solid waste is produced. In addition to any legal obligations that the Widget Factory has to change its production methods to minimize its environmental impact, what, if any, moral duty does it have to do so? Where do those obligations come from? If the company's manufacturing process is detrimental to the health of its workers or of people living in the area, should it continue to use that process? If so, under what restrictions? What level of risk is permissible, considering that almost every job involves some degree of danger? If there is no alternative method of production that the Widget Factory can use to make its product, does this mean that the product simply should not be made? If the product were a drug that is the only effective cure for a given disease, would environmental concerns take lower precedence?

What should the role of government be in assuring that corporations follow certain environmental standards? What other agencies might play a role in such enforcement?

3. Civic responsibility

What obligations do municipal, state, and federal governments have to make public transportation more accessible and efficient regardless

71

of the cost? Who should bear the cost of these changes? Should there be taxes on cars to pay for public transportation and to help lower emissions? What forms of energy should the city use for its own offices, for schools, and for other public facilities? High taxes often discourage businesses from moving to certain areas. How should a government balance the need to protect the environment with the need to foster economic development and protect jobs?

Traditional Sources

Compiled by Uzi Weingarten and the Editors

Individual Level

1. Genesis 2:15

The LORD God took the man and placed him in the garden of Eden, to till it and tend it.

2. Genesis 1:28–29

God blessed them and God said to them, "Be fertile and increase, fill the earth and master it; and rule the fish of the sea, the birds of the sky, and all the living things that creep on earth." God said, "See, I give you every seed-bearing plant that is upon all the earth, and every tree that has seed-bearing fruit; they shall be yours for food."

3. Genesis 9:1, 3

God blessed Noah and his sons, and said to them, "Be fertile and increase, and fill the earth … Every creature that lives shall be yours to eat; as with the green grasses, I give you all these."

4. Babylonian Talmud, *Bava Kamma* 50b

The Rabbis taught: A person should not clear stones from his property to public property. It happened that a person was clearing stones from his property to public property. A pious person met him and said: "Fool! Why are you clearing stones from property that is not yours to property that is yours?" [The owner of the field] mocked him.

Some time later he needed to sell his field, and [after that] he was walking in the same public place and tripped on those same stones. He said: That pious person spoke well when he asked me, "Why are you clearing stones from a place that is not yours to a place that is?"

5. Midrash, *Kohelet Rabbah* 7:19

When the Holy Blessed One created the first human, he took him and showed him all the trees of the Garden of Eden, and said to him: "See my creations, how beautiful and praiseworthy they are, and all that I have created, I created for you. Be mindful not to ruin and destroy my world, for if you ruin it, there is nobody to fix it after you."

6. Midrash, *Vayikra Rabbah* 16:3

From the beginning of the creation of the world, the Holy Blessed One was involved first only with planting, as it is written: "The Lord God planted a garden in Eden" (Genesis 2:8). You too, when you enter the Land, don't begin with anything other than planting, as it is written, "When you enter the Land and plant" (Leviticus 19:23).

Corporate Level
7. Mishnah, *Bava Batra* 2:1, 3 (Babylonian Talmud, *Bava Batra* 17a)

[1] One may not dig a well near his neighbor's well, nor a channel, cave, aqueduct, or basin for washing, unless he distanced it at least three spans from his neighbor's wall, and plastered with lime.

One must distance olive or poppy waste, dung, salt, lime, and flint-stones three spans from his neighbor's wall, and plaster with lime.

One must distance seeds, plowing, and urine from the wall three hand-lengths.

[3] One may not establish a bakery or a dyer's shop under his fellow's granary; and also not a stable for cattle.

[Regarding] a store in a courtyard, one can object and say, "I cannot sleep because of the noise of people entering and leaving."

But [the store owner] may make utensils and sell in the market, and one cannot object and say, "I cannot sleep from the noise of the hammer or the mill or the school children."

8. Joseph Caro, *Shulchan Arukh, Hoshen ha-Mishpat* 155:10

One may not dig a well near his neighbor's well, nor a channel, cave, aqueduct ... so that the waters not be absorbed and damage his fellow's wall.

9. Moses Isserles, gloss to *Shulchan Arukh, Hoshen ha-Mishpat* 155:20

[Regarding all] damage-causing things that are not spelled out [in the traditional sources], the extent of distancing is so that they not damage, according to expert opinion.

10. Joseph Caro, *Shulchan Arukh, Hoshen ha-Mishpat* 155:22, 34

One must distance a permanent threshing-floor fifty cubits from the city, so that the wind does not blow the straw during the threshing and cause damage to the city dwellers. Similarly, one may not make a permanent threshing-floor in his own property unless he has fifty cubits in each direction, so that the straw does not damage his neighbor's plantings or plowed field.

One who makes a threshing-floor in his property, or a restroom, or work that produces dust or dirt, etc. must distance them so that the dirt or smell of the restroom or the dust not reach another and harm him. Even if the wind assisted him at the time he was working, and carried the dirt or chaff and brought them to another, he must distance [his work] so that [these hazards] not reach his fellow and not harm him. All [damages caused by these hazards] are his direct damage (for which he is legally responsible even though the wind assisted).

11. Moses Isserles (16th century, Poland), gloss to *Shulchan Arukh, Hoshen ha-Mishpat* 155:31

If the harm does not come at the time of the work, but only later, then the one injured must distance himself [and is legally responsible for any injury he or she suffers].

Civic Level
12. Babylonian Talmud, *Bava Batra* 11a

R. Huna inquired of R. Ammi: If a man residing in one alleyway desires to open a door on to another alleyway, can the residents of this alleyway prevent him or not? He replied: They can prevent him … It has been taught to the same effect: The dung in the courtyard is divided according to doors [belonging to each resident, so that each can benefit from the fertilizer].

13. Maimonides (Rambam), *Mishneh Torah*, Laws of Neighbors 6:1

Residents of a city may obligate each other to build a wall, doors and locks for the city, and to build a synagogue, and to buy a Torah scroll, and Prophets and Writings (i.e., the rest of the Bible), so that whoever wishes to read may read.

Contemporary Sources

Compiled by Steven Edelman-Blank and Julia Oestreich

Individual Level

1. **Dan Fink, "Shabbat and the Sabbatical Year" in** *Ecology and the Jewish Spirit: When Nature and the Sacred Meet,* **Ellen Bernstein, ed. (Woodstock, VT: Jewish Lights, 1998), 116**

   Shabbat, a day that sets realistic limits on our consumption, has never been more vital than it is now. We need its commanding voice, which reminds us to walk lightly upon our planet. By revitalizing Shabbat, the Jewish people can help lead the way for all people toward increased ecological awareness. We can set an example by avoiding environmentally harmful types of work traditionally prohibited on Shabbat (such as driving and the unrestricted use of electricity) and creating new Shabbat observances (such as eating vegetarian meals, conserving water, and reducing waste).

2. **Tsvi Blanchard, "Can Judaism Make Environmental Policy? Sacred and Secular Language in Jewish Ecological Discourse" in** *Judaism and Ecology: Created World and Revealed Word,* **Hava Tirosh-Samuelson, ed. (Cambridge, MA: Center for the Study of World Religions, Harvard Divinity School, 2002), 424–25**

   Finally, in contemporary discussion, the impact and worth of religious and theological language are still being critically examined. For example, in the Hebrew Bible, God creates both nature and the human species. He then commands a relationship between them that, it has been alleged, can only be construed as one of human domination over nature. This alleged dominating, rule-over-it biblical attitude toward nature has recently been suggested as the root of our environmentally destructive policies. This would seem to make the Jewish tradition part of the problem, not the solution. Ironically, the biblical understanding of creation as sacred has also been offered as an antidote to what are seen as the destructive aspects of instrumental reason and its dominating relationship to nature. The latter reading of the Hebrew Bible complements a call for change in ecological consciousness as part of a solution to the present environmental crisis.

3. **Jeremy Benstein, *The Way Into Judaism and the Environment* (Woodstock, VT: Jewish Lights, 2006), 231–32**

To the long list of values and commitments that define the ideal Jew, we need to add being environmentally aware and active—for our own and our children's sakes, and for the sake of the *olam* (world) desperately in need of *tikkun*.

But on a deeper plane, the environment is not an issue to be added to our already overburdened catalog of causes; it is a perspective, a world view ...

There is also more that you can *do* yourself. There has been enormous creative initiative in Jewish environmental groups, but there is still potential to be fulfilled: greening your synagogue, setting up a study group ... changing personal and family lifestyles, connecting to organizations at home and in Israel that engage these issues, and more.

4. **Arthur Green, "To Work It and Guard It: Preserving God's World" in *Torah of the Earth: Exploring 4000 Years of Ecology in Jewish Thought*, Vol. 2, Arthur Waskow, ed. (Woodstock, VT: Jewish Lights, 2000), 202–03**

We must stop being callous and excessive users of earth's resources. We must become aware and share with others the realization that a small minority of the human race consumes far more than its appropriate share of earth's resources. We need to concern ourselves with the continued availability for generations to come of pure air, pure water, and good earth that will yield untainted produce. As good Jewish parents, concerned always with providing for our children, we must not allow ourselves to consume the legacy that belongs to future generations. The many areas in which to become active in ways helpful to the world's survival hardly need enumerating here. Each of us must find significant means to become partners in giving attention to such concerns. The fact that we band together in such activities with persons of good will who relate to the divine through other traditions (or without the language of traditional religion), is all for the good.

5. Jonathan Sacks, *To Heal a Fractured World: The Ethics of Responsibility* (New York: Schocken Books, 2005), 7–8

Global warming is not the result of one person using leaded petrol or an aerosol spray, but of billions of acts distributed throughout the world. The effects of environmental damage caused by the destruction of rain forests or over-exploitation of non-renewable energy sources may not be apparent during our lifetimes. Where then is my responsibility? My acts are less than a drop in the ocean of humanity. What I do or refrain from doing has an infinitesimal effect on the rest of the world. What duties do I have to something as amorphous as humanity in general, as inanimate as nature, or as intangible as generations not yet born? Any simple notion of responsibility is inadequate to such problems, which is why religious responsibility—responsibility to the infinite in terms of space, eternal in terms of time—can be more cogent than secular alternatives (not, I hasten to add, that religious individuals are more environmentally active than their secular counterparts: we all know the problem and we all try to help).

Communal Level

6. Mark X. Jacobs, "Jewish Environmentalism: Past Accomplishments and Future Challenges" in *Judaism and Ecology: Created World and Revealed Word*, Hava Tirosh-Samuelson, ed. (Cambridge, MA: Center for the Study of World Religions, Harvard Divinity School, 2002), 459

In most quarters, the environment is now considered an appropriate issue for Jewish concern. As a result, support for Jewish environmental education and action programs is increasingly widespread. There remains very limited, but influential, opposition to public Jewish action to address environmental challenges, particularly among two groups: community lay leadership, who often have business interests that conflict with an environmental agenda; and leaders who believe that the Jewish community should expend its resources and political capital on parochial issues of paramount concern to the Jewish community. Much of the growing support among Jewish leaders for a Jewish environmental program is a result of the capacity of environmental programs to involve Jews who might otherwise not be involved in Jewish communal life.

7. **Meir Tamari, *"With All Your Possessions": Jewish Ethics and Economic Life* (New York: The Free Press, 1987), 294**

All too often, even where there is physical damage involved, the economic welfare of the community would be seriously harmed by the removal of an offending plant or industry. If the damage envisaged is one that causes bodily harm, as distinct from inconvenience or irritation, the economic loss is not allowed to take precedence over the paramount concern for the safety of human beings.

8. **Arthur Waskow, "And the Earth is Filled with the Breath of Life," in *Torah of the Earth: Exploring 4000 Years of Ecology in Jewish Thought,* Vol. 2, Arthur Waskow, ed. (Woodstock, VT: Jewish Lights, 2000), 279**

For indeed the Jewish community, acting on its own, cannot heal the world. I could say to myself all day, "Hey, every time you drive the car you are polluting the planet and bringing on global warning," and yet if my society is set up so that the only way I can get from where I live to where I work is to drive, and there are no bike paths, and mass transit is rare, run-down, and expensive, then I am going to feel guilty but I am going to drive the car.

It does not help the planet if I feel guilty.

In other words, we have to act with other peoples and other communities to shape a society where we can walk from where we work to where we sleep, or we can bike, or we can take mass transit that is far more efficient and less wasteful and less likely to damage the atmosphere.

And we have to draw on the energy and clout of the Jewish people, our new ability in the Diaspora to make a difference in the societies we are a part of.

Civic Level

9. Eliezer Diamond, "How Much is Too Much? Conventional Versus Personal Definitions of Pollutions in Rabbinic Sources" in *Judaism and Ecology: Created World and Revealed Word*, Hava Tirosh-Samuelson, ed. (Cambridge, MA: Center for the Study of World Religions, Harvard Divinity School, 2002), 76

Although there is some debate about the degree of the danger and its causes, it is generally acknowledged that the planet's temperature is rising gradually, that this is due in part to our constant production of carbon dioxide, and that the potential results of continued warming could be catastrophic ...

Now comes the hard part. In order to avoid this scenario we need to reduce fossil fuel emissions significantly. The problem is: Who is going to do the reducing and by how much? The developing countries argue that the Western countries are producing much more carbon dioxide than they are and are much more able to absorb the financial costs of reducing emissions. The Western countries argue that the burden must be borne by all. If one were to adopt *halakhah's* preference for conventionality, which position would one support?

Although on its face the Western position of shared burdens may seem to be the more conventionally oriented one, we must recall the economic basis for *halakhah's* stance. A halakhist might turn to Western leaders and say, "Would you be willing to accept for yourselves the level of economic hardship that will be imposed on the developing nations if they accept the levels of emissions control you are demanding? If not, you ought to be ready to compensate them for economic losses sustained as a result or to agree to shift more of the reductions to yourselves, given that you are more able to sustain such reductions financially."

10. Jeremy Benstein, *The Way Into Judaism and the Environment* (Woodstock, VT: Jewish Lights, 2006), 130

The underlying question is one of individual convenience or advancement versus the collective good. Traditional societies, Judaism included, held to a different level of private responsibilities for public welfare. The environmentalist emphasis on the need for strong personal commitment and clear legislation protecting public welfare—even at the expense of curtailing certain primitive free-market notions of commercial liberty—speaks a common language of concern with the Torah.

Responses

Teshuvah to *Shylah*: Creating Questions from Answers

Arthur Waskow

F OR ALL of the questions in this case study, two teachings arise for me as transcendently important:

One is the contemporary consensus of the Intergovernmental Panel on Climate Change,[1] a council of scientists from around the world, that planet Earth is becoming overheated, that this poses very serious dangers to human civilization and to the web of life in which the human race came into existence, and that this process is mostly due to the actions of the human race itself.

The second is the warning in ancient passages in Leviticus 26:31–35 and 26:43 that failure to let the Earth rest, as described in Leviticus 25, will bring about social and ecological calamity: famine, drought, and exile. Leviticus is, I think, encoding the accumulated experience of farmers, shepherds, and orchard-keepers on the western edge of the Mediterranean as sacred wisdom.

These are the sharpest and most poignant teachings, but not the only relevant ones. The traditional second paragraph of the *Shema*, for example, taken from Deuteronomy 11:13–21, warns that if we follow the sacred teachings that flow from the One Who/That is the Unity of all life, then the rain, the soil, the sun, and the seed will unite to make our herds and our crops prosper and we will live well; but that if we turn to "afterthought gods" (*Elohim acherim*), then the earth, the river, and the sky will become our enemies. For me, the God of forethought, of flow, of the

---

1. The Intergovernmental Panel on Climate Change is a panel of scientists from all over the world, set up by two U.N. agencies—the World Meteorological Organization and the U.N. Environment Programme. The Panel consults all available scientific research on climate change and issues public reports (most recently in 2007) reflecting the views of its member scientists. Its reports have warned that major changes in world climate are resulting from human actions that increase the proportions of carbon dioxide and methane in the atmosphere. It shared the 2007 Nobel Peace Prize with former Vice President of the United States Al Gore.

Whole, is YHWH, Whose name cannot be pronounced but only breathed, because God is the interbreathing of all life. (Try pronouncing these four aspirate letters with no vowels, so not "Yahweh" or "Jehovah." For many people, what emerges is a breath or the sound of the wind. As the prayer book says, "*Nishmat kol chai tivarekh et shimkha*": The breath of all life praises Your Name." Thus, the Name replicates the interbreathing of all life.)

For me, these teachings are not sacred just because they are embedded in what we call Torah. They are sacred because they embody lived and living experience. And they point to what I can see around me: that human action can despoil, and is despoiling, our earth. Human beings, as well as entire species, are dying as a result.

Our story of Eden, the Garden of Delight, says that God shows us a world filled with abundance, and God says not to consume it all, but to practice self-restraint by choosing not to eat from one tree among the many. If we overuse it, the abundance will wither, the earth will give forth only thorns and thistles, and we will need to work with the sweat pouring down our faces in order to survive instead of enjoying the planet we have been given.

So, for me, modern scientists are simply specifying the terms of interconnection between *adamah* and *adam*, earth and earthling when they warn of the consequences of global warming. For each individual, and for corporations and governments, that connection produces the imperative to prevent the destruction of our world. To do so, we must limit our consumption of the abundance all around us.

Specifically, we must calm and cool our planet from the surplus of carbon dioxide and methane that is overheating it. We must move from burning fossil fuels to using "a sun of responsible justice (*shemesh tzedakah*) ... with healing in its wings" (Mal. 3:20): solar energy and the *ruach hakodesh*—the "holy wind" that is moved each day by the healing wings of that sun. We must also restrain our consumption of meat, whose production pours methane into our atmosphere.

And we especially must take upon ourselves the task that Malachi invokes with Elijah: to turn the hearts of parents and children to each other lest the earth be utterly destroyed in the coming of an "awesome, fearful day" that burns "like an oven." (Mal. 3:19, 23–24). We can fulfill this task by using the time when our children become bar/bat mitzvah, a time when education and ceremony focus on committing each generation to the next, to work on healing our earth from the climate crisis we have brought upon it.[2]

It is also important to pursue the hands-on practices of an "eco-kosher" life-path, in which not only food but everything else we "eat" from the earth—like coal and oil—must be consumed in a way that seeks to heal the Earth. Perhaps even more importantly, it is necessary for Jews to advocate vigorously for changes in public policy. It has become clear that governments will take effective action on the climate crisis only if the public insists on serious change.

I encourage action based on the following seven principles, which are deeply rooted in Jewish tradition, and which should act as a yardstick for measuring the success and integrity of Jewish and interfaith efforts to shape U.S. and world policy on the climate crisis:[3]

1. Our planet has always been a living demonstration that "**the Breathing Spirit of the universe is One**" ("YHWH *Ehad*"), but the climate crisis gives us the clearest awareness of that truth. The planet is in this as One. Policy must reflect that. This underlying Jewish principle is expressed in the *Shema*, especially in the traditional second paragraph on rain and crops.

2. **The cost to those responsible for spewing CO_2 and methane into the atmosphere must be greatly increased** through taxation and/or "cap and trade" legislation that requires payment from carbon producers according to the damage they are causing. The underlying Jewish principle here is captured in Exodus 21:28–30:

> When an ox gores a man or a woman to death, the ox shall be stoned and its flesh shall not be eaten, but the owner of the ox is not to be punished. If, however, that ox has been in the habit of goring, and its owner, though warned, has failed to guard it, and it kills a man or a woman—the ox shall be stoned and its owner, too, shall be put to death. If ransom is laid upon him, he must pay whatever is laid upon him to redeem his life.

---

2. See The Shalom Center's "Elijah's Covenant Between the Generations" as one approach to doing this. Available at http://www.shalomctr.org/node/1363.

3. This list was originally published in an article: Arthur Waskow, "Climate Policy: 7 Principles & a Yardstick," Oct. 30, 2009. Available at http://www.theshalomcenter.org/node/1588.

3. The pool of money these measures bring in must be used to lower or control the high costs of fuel and energy that hurt the poor and the middle class. Additionally, **this climate healing fund should be used for rebates**, with more used for the poorest people. Jewish principles of tithing, gleaning, and obligatory *tzedakah* to assist the poor, orphans, widows, and the landless apply here.

4. Big Coal and Big Oil have great political power, but their power must be limited, **so they cannot distort necessary policy as they try to expand their own power and profits**. For instance, the Environmental Protection Agency must continue to have power to enforce CO_2 limits on coal-burning power plants, even though Big Coal is using every form of influence and pressure to blunt the agency's power. The behavior of the coal and oil lobbies reminds us of resistance to top-down unaccountable powers—such as Pharaoh, Antiochus, and the Romans—in Jewish history.

5. Inside the U.S., industries and regions that are especially threatened by energy reform (e.g., coal mining, oil drilling, the auto industry) must be given special help for **retraining employees in green jobs**. Maimonides' eighth and highest approach to *tzedakah* can provide a model: help the poor to end their own poverty by providing capital, etc., as in giving them a fishing rod, not just a fish.

6. Outside the U.S., **poor nations must be given major help** by first-world countries for two purposes: to pursue economic development through fossil fuel alternatives and to meet urgent crises already creating natural disasters for them. Maimonides' eighth *tzedakah* principle also applies here.

7. Public policy must start encouraging what we usually think of as "personal" choices to engage in practices that don't harm the environment: **setting aside much more restful and reflective time for family and community, and much less "production/consumption" time**. Ways to encourage this shift include being frugal in our energy use; eating less meat; living simple lifestyles; allocating more money for education, the arts, etc. and less for producing things; raising

taxes, subsidies, and wages; and passing laws for more favorable work hours and conditions. Shabbat provides an example from the Jewish tradition of a practice (that is earth-healing as well as human-healing) that demonstrates communal commitment, not just individual choice.

Out of these principles, I suggest the following list of questions as a yardstick for measuring proposed U.S. policies (and by extension, those of other governments):

Do they promote American energy independence and security, and the healing of our planet by:

- immediately ending all government subsidies for the production of oil and coal?

- radically and swiftly reducing the burning of oil and coal from all sources, foreign and domestic?

- simultaneously using all possible measures to build an energy base for the American economy on solar, wind, and other sources of waste-free, sustainable energy while taking urgent steps for energy conservation?

- making the creation of "green jobs" and green infrastructure the central focus of a transition to a new American economy?

- giving aid to poor nations to pursue a path outside of fossil-fuel production for economic and social development?

In many of the festivals and life-cycle moments marked in Jewish life, there are direct applications of profound teachings and practices that encourage us to heal the earth and its climate. For example, forests are crucial to maintaining the oxygen/carbon dioxide balance in our planetary atmosphere. So Tu b'Shvat celebrations might be focused on that urgent need. Hanukkah recalls that one day's oil was enough for eight days. So that holiday might help us focus on reducing the use of fossil fuels and on conserving energy.

To broaden our commitments as Jews to implementing hands-on changes at personal, household, and congregational levels, and to helping make the necessary changes at regional, national, and international levels, we must fulfill specific obligations. They might include the following:[4]

1. *The costs of carbon*:

Personal change: setting aside 5% of annual household coal, oil, and gasoline costs for *tzedakah* (contributions on behalf of social responsibility) to support sustainable-energy activism.

Public policy: requiring energy producers to pay for the carbon emissions their products cause through a carbon tax, carbon cap-and-invest laws, or a combination thereof.

2. *Energy*:

Personal change: buying energy-conserving appliances for households, joining wind energy plans, etc.

Public policy: ending subsidies for such carbon-producing sources of energy as coal, oil, and corn-based ethanol and increasing subsidies for such non-carbon-emitting sources of energy as wind, solar, and switch-grass.

3. *Buildings*:

Personal change: greening new homes and congregations, and retro-greening present buildings.

Public policy: enacting strong environmentally conscious building codes for constructing new buildings and for retrogreening old ones.

4. *Transportation*:

Personal change: car-pooling, walking, or biking as households and congregations to jobs, synagogues/churches, etc.

Public policy: ending subsidies for buying conventional automobiles, constructing highways, and for the airline industry; strictly limiting emissions for automobiles and airplanes; raising subsidies for bikes, rail travel, and holding long-distance meetings by teleconference.

---

4. This list was originally published in an article: Arthur Waskow, "Green Menorah Covenant Coalition: Personal, Congregational, & Public Policy Changes to Avert Global Scorching," Nov. 19, 2009. Available at http://www.theshalomcenter.org/node/1276.

5. *Land use*:

Personal change: urban-style high-density living (whether in actual cities or in suburbs).

Public Policy: subsidizing and investing in urban recreation, workplaces, etc. instead of in sprawl and low-density housing.

6. *Food*:

Personal change: choosing locally grown food (supporting local agriculture, minimizing transportation-caused burning of fossil fuels); restricting eating meat from methane-producing animals to once a week.

Public Policy: taxing beef; requiring that cattle be fed on grass (to produce less methane); taxing long-distance food transport; subsidizing local farms.

7. *Education and ritual*:

Personal change: infusing festivals, life-cycle events (especially intergenerational markers like bar/bat mitzvah and confirmation), prayer, and Torah study with concern for the earth and climate.

Public policy: subsidizing scientific climate crisis analysis; creating climate-centered curricula for students from pre-Kindergarten through graduate school; supporting art, literature, music, dance, film, games, etc. that address the climate crisis.

8. *Shabbat and restful time*:

Personal change: strongly encouraging setting aside restful time—even more than before—in individual and congregational practice and making minimal use of carbon-emitting energy during Shabbat itself, as a wise and sacred Jewish practice.

Public policy: requiring paid leave to be allotted for parental care and holiday time to be set aside for neighborhood-centered celebration.

If the Jewish community and other American faith communities undertake the task of making changes to help the environment in all the dimensions mentioned here, our lives as a whole can become a practice of rededicating and reconsecrating the temple of God's Presence: Earth.

Preventing Our Stumble

Justin Goldstein

A N INTERESTING *aggadah*, a moral tale, appears in tractate *Bava Kamma*[1] of the Babylonian Talmud. It reads:

> The Rabbis taught: A person should not clear stones from his property to public property. It happened that a person was clearing stones from his property to public property. A pious person met him and said: "Fool! Why are you clearing stones from property that is not yours to property that is yours?" [The owner of the field] mocked him. Some time later he needed to sell his field, and [after that] he was walking in the same public place and tripped on those same stones. He said: That pious person spoke well when he asked me, "Why are you clearing stones from a place that is not yours to a place that is?"

This tale raises a few interesting points. First, it might seem counterintuitive that the person's private property is "property that is not yours," as described by the pious individual's chastising. This is one of the many ways in which the Jewish tradition reminds us that God is the true owner of the Earth, and we are its inhabitants and stewards.[2]

The man clearing stones is being inconsiderate to his community by littering in the public area. The idea that he is part of that community is clearly shown when he trips over his mess. Thus, when we "clear stones" into the public domain, we are not only harming others, we are also harming ourselves. If we, as individuals, purchase products that are harmful to the environment or support companies that are unnecessarily destructive, we become party to environmental destruction.

In this parable, the stones can be read as our abuse of the environment. The man clearing stones is each and every one of us, and is also most corporations. The pious individual represents our collective conscience,

---

1. This version is taken from the Babylonian Talmud, *Bava Kamma* 50b. There is a more drawn out version in the Tosefta, *Bava Kamma* 2:10.
2. The concept of the Land of Israel as the "Promised Land" is one in which God is envisioned as a landlord, entrusting property to a tenant. Legal principles such as *shmitah* (the agricultural sabbatical year that occurs once every seven years) and *yovel* (the jubilee, which occurs every seven sabbatical years) highlight the structure under which we are just temporary owners.

reminding us that thoughtless waste and environmental wantonness have been responsible for widespread devastation in our natural ecosystem, causing clear, irreparable effects. It is impossible to ignore the fact that our choices and actions now affect us in more and more noticeable ways—in other words, we have, in a sense, "cluttered" our public domain by actively and passively participating in harming our environment.

Placing a Stumbling Block

This story implicitly alludes to the important commandment from the Torah: *lifnei i'ver lo titein mikhshol*, "You shall not … place a stumbling block before the blind" (Lev. 19:14). The rabbinic tradition has understood this prohibition to refer to a ban on assisting Jews in transgressing *mitzvot* ("commandments"). For example, a Jewish business owner is prohibited from selling products forbidden to other Jews, such as idols or non-kosher foods.[3] The buyer, who does not know whether or not an item is forbidden (and is thus "blind"), might mistakenly think that, since it is sold by a Jew, it is kosher. Thus, its presence in the store serves as a "stumbling block."

In regard to the environment, and consumer responsibility, I like to employ the principal of *lifnei iver* in an unconventional sense. We live in a market-driven economy. In very simple terms, what we buy determines what is sold. Many companies produce goods people want that have a negative environmental impact, which may include obvious things, such as air pollution or increased carbon output. However, there are other unseen impacts of consumer decisions. Despite these negative environmental consequences, companies in our society tend to choose making a profit over sustaining the environment.[4] As consumers in a market-driven economy, we have power within that structure and therefore, we have responsibility.

---

3. For example, in the 19th century, the Rabbi Avraham Shmuel Binyamin Sofer (Ketav Sofer) wrote, "If he does not own it and must thus purchase it, then perhaps even if it is available for him to buy, '*lifnei iver*' would apply." Babylonian Talmud, *Yoreh De'ah* 83.

4. On March 28, 2001, then President George W. Bush explained that he was pulling out of the international treaty on climate change known as the Kyoto Protocol by saying, "I will not accept anything that will harm our economy or hurt our American workers." President Bush had insistently opposed any reduction of greenhouse emissions according to the terms of the Kyoto Protocol because he argued that would "destroy our economy." His statement may or may not be true, yet it clearly showed an unwillingness to reduce profit margins in the name of environmental stewardship.

If a Jewish store owner provides items forbidden to Jewish individuals, and a Jewish consumer unknowingly purchases one of those products, that store owner may be guilty of *lifnei iver*. When we buy products or support companies that unnecessarily harm the environment, are we not giving these companies an incentive to continue with "business as usual"? Although this is not the traditional application of *lifnei iver*, by providing profit for a company despite their engagement in irreparable, unnecessary environmental destruction, we become party to a greed-driven system and thus perhaps guilty of placing stumbling blocks in front of others.

Individual Choices and Global Implications

Clearly, our consumer choices are informed by many more considerations than environmental impact alone. What's more, we do not always know when a company is being environmentally irresponsible in the name of profit. There are, however, simple steps that each of us can take that may seem inconsequential, but can, in fact, have significant impact on the environment. For example, by opting to bring our own bags or baskets to the grocery store so that we do not need to use plastic or paper bags to take our food home, we can help reduce greenhouse emissions, landfill toxicity, and foreign dependency on oil.

Another step we can take concerns meat consumption. One of the most environmentally damaging industries today is the meat industry. Greenhouse gasses emitted from livestock, from cow and industrial waste and from farming equipment, not to mention the overuse of grazing land, have created an unsustainable process. Whether animals are slaughtered in a kosher way or not, they are usually raised on the same farms that participate in that process. Therefore, when we consume the products of the factory-farm meat industry, we aid environmental destruction.[5] It would, therefore, be wise to reduce or eliminate meat from our diet; but if one feels compelled to maintain a meat-heavy diet, it would be best for the environment to consider eating grass-fed, free-range products.[6]

---

5. *Livestock's Long Shadow: Environmental Issues and Options*, Livestock, Environment and Development (Rome: Food and Agriculture Organization of the United Nations, 2006). Available at http://www.fao.org/docrep/010/a0701e/a0701e00.HTM.

6. One of the most devastating aspects of industrialized meat production is the amount of food and water that must be allocated to livestock instead of to people. An overwhelming amount of corn is grown not for human consumption, but to be eaten by livestock raised for slaughter. Buying meat from grass-fed animals is a way to avoid being part of the destructive cycle of waste.

Perhaps the most meaningful thing that people can do for our environment as consumers, is to purchase environmentally friendly products. When we invest our resources in such products, companies are given incentive to produce more of them. Over the last 50 years, the United States has evolved into a consumer culture focused on disposables. We use plastic bottles, plastic baggies, plastic wrap, and plastic boxes, all produced with the intent to be thrown away after one use. In addition to plastic disposables, we see incredible amounts of paper wasted in the name of packaging. Our packaging problem has gotten so out of hand that, according to the Environmental Protection Agency, the majority of our landfills are made up of paper products.[7] Much of that paper comes from packaging, and the source of paper is, as we know, trees. By supporting companies that use 100% post-consumer recycled products for their packaging, we can reduce massive deforestation in the U.S. and abroad. In this way, we can help to save diverse ecosystems that assure the proper balance in our planet's ecology and can help prevent, and even counteract, climate change. By ultimately choosing to purchase environmentally friendly consumer goods, we can drive the market to produce more of them.

Corporate Responsibility

We must also take care not to buy from a company that plunders and pollutes the environment for profit. If a major international corporation—for example, Coca-Cola—packages its products in recycled and recyclable materials, that act is not enough to offset that corporation's industrial practices if they are causing widespread environmental damage.[8]

---

7. See the Environmental Protection Agency's Wastes website at http://www.epa.gov/epawaste/index.htm.
8. In India, Coca-Cola has been accused of using rural villages' ground water to produce its beverages, in effect drying the wells of these communities. The bottling process then produces waste that is discarded back into the water of some of these communities, leaving remaining fresh water sources too polluted to consume or use for agriculture. Paul Brown, "Coca-Cola in India Accused of Leaving Farms Parched and Land Poisoned," *The Guardian,* July 25, 2003. Available at http://www.guardian.co.uk/environment/2003/jul/25/water.india. In the 1990s, McDonalds was engaged in a long trial defending itself against accusations of rainforest destruction. While Jewish consumers who keep kosher are not customers of McDonalds, its practices demonstrate that the negative impacts of rainforest destruction are global in scale. "McDonald's Linked to Rainforest Destruction," *World Rainforest Report*, Rainforest Information Centre, June 1, 1996. Available at http://forests.org/archive/general/macfore.htm.

Consumer responsibility is incredibly important to environmental protection, but clearly corporate responsibility is just as vital. Therefore, consumers must take it upon themselves to pressure corporations to protect the environment in developing nations that may not have legislative protections in place.

It is no secret that corporations abuse their rights and privileges.[9] Where do corporations fit into the Talmud parable I quoted at the start of this essay? Business growth is a necessary component of a free market society. Using the concept broadly, unnecessary pollution is like "clearing stones." Yet, we must be sensitive to the necessity of a business to profit and succeed. Typically, in business, growth equals increased profit. Unfortunately, resources are limited—as we've painfully learned in America's attempt to reduce its dependency on oil—and growth produces environmental destruction as well. The teaching in the Talmud, "A person should not clear stones from his property to public property," is very vague. It leaves one wondering: Should one not clear stones under *any* circumstances? May one dispose of stones in the public domain if he or she places them with care and has an awareness of their impact?

Waste is unavoidable, whether it is tied to the production of paper, energy, or something else. That said, does the Jewish tradition allow for unnecessary waste and abuse in order to sustain profit and business growth? In other words, does the Jewish tradition permit a business to knowingly harm the environment? In the earliest teachings of Jewish law, rights are accorded to businesses that may not be accorded to others. For example, a Mishnah in *Bava Batra* 2:3 reads, "The noise of a smith's hammer, of a mill, or of children in school, is not to be considered a nuisance." This is found amid a series of rulings regarding how two neighboring properties must strive to reduce damage and nuisance to each other. The Mishnah recognizes that it is in the nature of the hammer, mill, or schoolhouse to be noisy. Likewise, we must recognize that some businesses will have to pollute and produce unwanted waste. It is also important to recognize that many products are essential parts of our lives and are things that society collectively needs or desires, such as medicines

---

9. From Enron to Agriprocessors, from widespread environmental destruction to widespread fraud, corruption scandals in business are an ever-increasing aspect of our world. There are many ways in which today's corporations shirk their responsibility to protect the environment.

and automobiles, making them worth a certain amount of environmental harm.

The parable in *Bava Kamma* reminds us that while we each have our own interests and priorities, our actions and decisions affect those around us. Corporations are ultimately made up of individuals, but each corporation that harms the environment actually harms its own employees and its own interests as a whole. Historically, however, this has not compelled corporations to pursue more sustainable products or methods of production. The goal of a sustainable community is not to eradicate business or dismiss its interests; rather, it is to find a balance between profit and a healthy, sustainable environment. In keeping with our parable, it is foolish for companies to pollute in such a way that even the individuals who make up the company are harmed, much as it was foolish for the man to clear stones onto public property, where he himself would eventually trip on them.

Often, there is industry-specific waste that affects specific communities, and sometimes that waste is unavoidable. For instance, one problem in contemporary food production is that of excess amounts of animal waste. Common practices for dairy and cattle farms to deal with this problem include using manure lagoons, which hold manure in lakes. In the chicken and egg industries, waste is often powdered and sprayed into the air with large, industrial fans. Manure spills have caused significant environmental damage, polluting water supplies and killing fish and other wildlife. Residents who live near egg and chicken farms are subject to noxious fumes and toxic residue from bacteria in the manure.[10]

Some of these concerns are a matter of scale. While the Jewish tradition is not opposed to profit, it is opposed to profiteering. For example, Maimonides ruled that a person should not make a profit that constitutes more than one-sixth of what he or she earns through his or her transactions.[11] Increasing the bottom line should thus never motivate an individual or a business to cut corners or engage in practices that may harm others. If the scale of a venture prohibits sustainable methods of

---

10. In 2001, 21 residents near Buckeye Egg Farm in Ohio were awarded $19 million in damages as a result of the widespread pollution caused by the farm's methods of manure disposal.

11. Maimonides, *Mishneh Torah*, Laws of Sale (*Hilkhot Mekhirah*) 13:1.

waste control, the environment and public should not suffer. Rather, in accord with the Jewish tradition of respecting profit, but not profiteering, the business should reform.

Reducing rates of production so that businesses could reduce the rate at which they used resources necessary for production would allow those resources to be used for longer periods of time, not only accommodating environmental sustainability, but also encouraging business growth over the long-term. Many large companies have sought alternatives to environmentally destructive practices. For example, Staples, the largest office supply chain in America, has committed itself to promoting the sale of 100% recycled paper, opting to phase out products made from endangered forests. It is true that reducing production rates might reduce immediate profit, but this should be tolerated and viewed as a necessary expense, unless it puts the business in danger of bankruptcy. In the end, a business benefits most from the type of growth that benefits all of its stakeholders, not from that which is aimed at feeding its owner's bank account. A business is capable of earning a profit without its owners engaging in profiteering.

Municipal Responsibility

According to the teaching from *Bava Kamma*, an individual should not clear objects from his or her own domain into the public domain. We have considered the interpretation that individual acts of polluting and the support of companies that pollute could amount to "clearing stones" into our public space and "placing stumbling blocks." Assuming that communities and municipalities also have the responsibility to not "clear stones" or "place stumbling blocks," at what point are they responsible to fund and provide environmentally sustainable development?

Municipalities work on budgets, often operating at a deficit. There is never enough funding to meet everyone's needs and desires. Yet there are steps that municipalities, large and small, can take to afford a more sustainable future and to make real changes now.

One major challenge regarding climate change is finding practical and sustainable land use policies. Cities and townships often favor development at the expense of residents and the environment. They certainly have a responsibility to cultivate economic production and business growth, but at what cost? There are ways that municipalities could encourage more appropriate land use by businesses without harming their capacity for production or growth. For example, some cities, states, and nations have decided to require that all new buildings be fitted with solar-powered water heaters, and that many large stores (such as supermarkets or retail chain locations) create their own energy with wind turbines and rooftop solar panels.[12]

Municipalities can also limit the cost and emissions of their public transportation systems by implementing benefits for carpoolers, such as designated lanes on highways, or by requiring that public busses and municipal vehicles be run at least partially on electricity or natural gas. Los Angeles, for example, already has the largest fleet of natural gas public busses in the country. Public transportation and solar panels will not end climate change, but they will allow cities to participate in helping the environment.

Ultimately, the Earth is our home and we must care for it. Jewish tradition implores us to steward it respectfully. Just as we must repair the foundations of our houses if they are cracked to assure the safety and security of our families and ourselves, we must also act to clean up humanity's home—a home whose future is threatened by what we have "cleared to public property."

---

12. In 2008, the State of Hawaii, following the lead of Israel and Spain, began requiring the use of solar water heaters in new homes. Since that time, companies such as Home Depot, Wal-Mart, and Whole Foods Market have also been producing some of their own energy at select locations.

Struggling with Environmental Balance

Joel S. Jacobs

Taking Personal Responsibility for a Problem You Cannot Solve

FORMER VICE President Dick Cheney famously commented that, "Conservation may be a sign of personal virtue, but it is not a sufficient basis for a sound, comprehensive energy policy."[1] Putting aside any doubts we may have about the second part of his comment, what about the first part? Is practicing conservation a sign of virtue, and what does that mean?

It is all too easy to mock individual efforts at conservation. Sadly, one person's choice to recycle or reduce consumption will not stop global warming. It won't plug the hole in the ozone layer. It won't even save a forest. Over enough time, it might save a tree, but what good is that if all the other trees around it are being chopped down? What is a well-meaning person to do?

I could just wait for the government to act in the hope that it will enact broad, systemic changes that will actually make a difference. Or, I could conserve resources on a personal level, not because my actions will change the world, but because my choices reflect the kind of person I want to be. They are also a way of being part of the world, and not apart from it.

Some people see the Earth's resources as existing for the benefit of humankind. I believe, however, that the *ability* to consume a resource is not the equivalent of the *right* to consume it. We all share the Earth, and we should aim to be good at sharing, with each other, with future generations, and with the Earth itself.

I can never know all of the consequences of my consumer decisions, but that doesn't mean I shouldn't consider those decisions carefully, with an eye toward their environmental impacts. When I was a boy, in Hebrew School we would often sing a song based on the Mishnah, *"Lo alekha ham'lakhah ligmor, v'lo atah ben horin l'hibatil mimenah"* ("It is not your duty to complete the work, but neither are you free to desist from it" [Avot 2:21]). It is easy for us to ignore a problem because we know that we cannot solve it on our own. Most environmental problems are so large that

---

1. Richard Benedetto, "Cheney's Energy Plan Focuses on Production," *USA Today,* May 1, 2001.

our small, individual actions cannot solve them or even make a noticeable dent in them. But for me, ignoring them because I cannot solve them feels like a copout. The problems are there. They are real, and they are quite serious. It can be overwhelming to deal with them, but we still live in a community, and we cannot run away from our obligations.

I trust my own decisions more when I try to think about their direct environmental consequences. For instance, the knowledge that cars pollute has not caused me to get rid of my car, but I do pause before hopping into it. Every mile I drive puts pollutants in the air. I think about those pollutants, and I ask myself what the alternatives are to driving. Usually I choose one of these alternatives: public transit, biking, walking, or carpooling. Sometimes I drive, but the more my actions are based on conscious choices, and the less they are based on habits, the more they match what I expect from myself.

Making conscious personal decisions to try to help the environment may make me feel better despite the world's failure to take the dramatic action necessary to tackle environmental challenges. Still, I believe that considering the consequences of my actions is the cornerstone of my personal morality. There are all kinds of calculators on the Internet that convert lifestyle decisions into estimates of our environmental footprints. They do not dictate particular choices, but they do facilitate more informed ones. A world made up of people who consider the potential environmental harm they may cause before they act is the kind of world I want to live in.

Corporate and Governmental Responsibility Toward the Environment

The law treats corporations as "persons," but the reality is much more complicated, of course. I do not believe that the moral obligations of corporations are the same as those of individuals. The question of whether businesses have moral obligations to incur costs in order to protect the environment is a very difficult one. In contrast, identifying the responsibility of government toward the environment is much easier.

Capitalism puts great pressure on businesses not to sacrifice profit for the environment. The extra costs that a company may voluntarily incur for environmentally conscious practices can put it at a competitive disadvantage against rival companies that are making less environmentally conscious choices. As a result, our society has made a collective decision that some level of environmental harm is acceptable from businesses. I would like companies to "do no harm," but that is often not possible if a business is to carry out its mission and remain competitive. And what should happen to a company that needs to pollute in order to make products that help people?

The environmental responsibilities of government are much clearer. Government has a central role to play in balancing the economic needs of businesses (and, by extension, of society) against the need to protect the health of citizens and the planet. Government can level the playing field so that all companies must follow the same rules and none can gain an economic advantage by adopting fewer measures to protect the environment than competitors. Government also has the power to punish those who violate the rules by imposing fines that, if set high enough and imposed with sufficient consistency, make following the law more attractive than ignoring it.

Government can overcome so-called "collective action problems," which, if everyone works together to solve them, can create benefits for all; but it is generally in the personal interest of each individual to ignore problems and let others deal with them. There is inherent incentive to be what economists call a "free rider," one who does not contribute to the common good, but benefits from others' contributions. Air pollution is a prime example of a collective action problem: everyone benefits if harmful emissions are reduced, but each person and company feels better off if they do not have to bear the costs of limiting emissions. Government is in the best position to attack collective action problems because it can make rules that apply to everyone, and it can enforce them. If it does so, no one has to get singled out as a target, but no one can be a free rider without breaking the law.

Because government has an obligation to protect people from harm, it must regulate air and water quality, emissions, workplace safety standards, and a host of other areas that affect industry and the community. Government, however, also has an obligation to promote economic activity, and therefore it cannot over-regulate to the point where it destroys productive, legal businesses. In addition to making rules and enforcing them, government must educate itself about environmental science and the market, and must rely on sound science for its decisions about how to strike a balance between these two forces. If technologies to control pollution are affordable and effective, government should require their usage.

Government regulation is not necessarily a zero-sum game in which each step that helps the public harms business. Companies tend to prefer market-based solutions, in which they can buy and sell credits for environmentally harmful activities (like air pollution), over "command and control" approaches, in which they are told what the limits on their activities are. On the other hand, companies and individuals often prefer specific instructions when there is uncertainty about how to achieve mandated goals. Given the choice between creating its own improvement program and paying a fee to support a government program, a company will often choose the latter. Companies like predictability; some environmental regulations are more manageable when the affected companies have been given advance notice. When obligations are clear and mandates are given with fair warning, compliance is easier, and everyone benefits.

Finally, evenhandedness and uniformity are critical, as well. If everyone is playing by the same rules, those rules are easier to accept, and the players can know that they are competing on a level playing field. Government should not use environmental regulation to bestow advantages on certain competitors in the marketplace (unless, of course, doing so creates incentives for instituting environmental protections).

In sum, the moral decisions of individuals and businesses can be colored by concerns about what others are doing. We may worry about being ineffectual or naïve when we make environmentally conscious choices that many of our peers do not. Government, on the other hand, can change the incentives for an entire community, state, or country with a single act. This is great power with potentially marvelous or catastrophic consequences.

The Example of Public Transportation

Just as government is uniquely positioned to act on environmental issues, it is also in the best position to make changes to public transportation. But does government have a moral obligation to provide public transit as part of its environmental policy?

My grandmother recently stopped driving, fearing she could no longer drive safely. The problem is, though, that in America, driving is freedom. For my grandmother, giving up her license has meant being far more dependent on others—going out only when she can get a ride from someone else or when the trip is important enough to justify paying for a cab. She now spends more time alone at home rather than out in her community, but accessible public transportation could help change that. She is certainly not the only person profoundly affected by whether public transit is available and convenient.

Public transit issues affect two groups of people, and there are different moral- and policy-related questions raised for each. There is one group of people—the elderly, children, disabled people, those who cannot afford cars, and those who never learned to drive—for whom driving is not an alternative to public transit. I believe that city, state, and federal governments have an obligation to them. After all, government offers assistance with food, housing, education, and other needs to those who have difficulty helping themselves. Transportation is also essential to modern life, as it is often necessary for holding a job, receiving medical care, going to school, and even buying groceries. Without good public transit, we are essentially cutting off the most vulnerable members of society from these activities; we are abandoning them.

The other group of people is, of course, those who can drive. They will arrive at their destinations one way or another; it is just a question of how. It is important to get them on public transit as well, not just for the quality of their own lives (good transit can help them travel more safely and productively, with less stress), but also for the sake of the environment.

This brings us to the more difficult question of how to pay for improving the quality and availability of public transportation. Because society as a whole has an obligation to those who cannot drive and to the health of our planet, it seems reasonable for some of our tax dollars to go to supporting public transit. It also seems reasonable to tax car use (through tolls, parking fees, gas taxes, etc.) and to use some of the generated revenue for public transit, as well. In fact, the additional revenue could pay for improvements that would make public transit more appealing, incentivizing those who drive to use it. This revenue could be directed toward other fiscal priorities, as well.

For too long, we have not paid enough attention to the true cost of driving a car. It is not just the cost of the gas, insurance, maintenance, and repairs. The true cost of driving a car includes both the cost of building and maintaining related infrastructure, as well as the health costs related to ailments caused by the pollution cars create. Although these costs can be difficult to measure, we should still discourage driving and make public transit as attractive as possible. The more people use public transit, the more cost-effective it will become.

Inadequate public transportation is also a collective action problem, as it requires a critical mass in order to implement an effective solution. Everyone wants a good public transit system, but few people want to use a poor existing system with the hope of helping the system grow. Yet, only when ridership is high enough will the incentives for individuals become more in sync with the incentives for society. And the more convenient public transit becomes, the more driving will lose some of its allure. Of course, high ridership on public transit requires population density, so while many public transit issues are financial (such as how much it costs and who pays), the land use policies that determine where people live, work, and shop are equally important. I am much more likely to use a train that stops a block away from my destination than one that may be clean and fast but does not go where I need it to. Cities and counties should pursue "smart growth," which promotes the development of urban centers with nearby transit.

Finally, every government needs to balance protecting the environment with promoting economic growth. Good mass transit can, in fact, promote such growth, revitalizing downtown areas, helping to create jobs, and saving money for businesses and workers. Yet, public transportation must not be limited to transit that pays for itself. Our moral obligations to fellow citizens require more than that, and so does our obligation to the environment.

Our duty, as individuals and as the citizens who empower our government, is to examine what meaningful steps we can take to protect and improve our community and our planet. We are not free to desist from it.

CASE 4

✃

CRIMINAL JUSTICE

Case Study

Criminal Justice

1. The Rationales and Forms of Punishment

What should be the aim of punishment? Should it be retribution, compensation, deterrence, rehabilitation, safety, or something else? Is prison the most effective way of achieving any of those goals, or should some mode of alternative punishment and/or preventive measures be the focus of our efforts to deal with crime?

Some jurisdictions are now using restorative justice programs, in which the perpetrators of property crimes meet their victims and have to enter into a contract with them to restore what was lost as part or all of their punishment. Should programs of restorative justice be implemented more widely than they are now? Is this approach sufficient to achieve the various goals of punishment?

Presumably, a punishment should fit the crime. Is that possible if some states punish certain crimes much more severely than others? Furthermore, the U.S. imprisons a much greater percentage of its citizens than any other Western country. How do we know that this is both an appropriate and effective way of addressing crime? How does one determine what an appropriate punishment for a crime is in the first place?

What percentage of state and federal budgets should be devoted to enforcing the law instead of to social needs like education, infrastructure, health care, welfare, culture, and so forth?

2. The Death Penalty

As of 2009, 15 U.S. states and most other fully developed countries do not have capital punishment. The arguments against capital punishment include: convicted individuals may be innocent; the cost of the appeals process in a capital case is too great; it makes the United States seem uncivilized to other countries who don't use the practice; human beings do not have the right to play God; it constitutes cruel and unusual punishment in violation of the Bill of Rights; it does not effectively deter crime; and it has been disproportionately applied to racial minorities and the poor.

The arguments for capital punishment include: it represents true justice in its eye-for-an-eye approach; it avenges both the victim and society; it protects society, preventing the convicted criminal from committing further crimes; it deters others from committing such crimes; by perpetrating a capital crime, the criminal implicitly consents to the death penalty; and it symbolically expresses the wrath of society in response to such crimes.

Although the Torah mandates capital punishment for many violations, including desecration of the Sabbath, the Rabbis used the rules of evidence and other legal mechanisms to virtually abrogate that mandate. In fact, the Mishnah (Mak. 1:10) calls a court that hands down a capital sentence just once in seven years, a "bloody court."

Is the use of capital punishment justified? Even if it can be justified, is it morally acceptable?

Traditional Sources

Compiled by Uzi Weingarten and the Editors

Forms of Punishment

1. Exodus 21:37, 22:3

When a man steals an ox or a sheep, and slaughters it or sells it, he shall pay five oxen for the ox, and four sheep for the sheep ... But if what he stole—whether ox or ass or sheep—is found alive in his possession, he shall pay double.

2. Rashi to Exodus 21:37

Rabban Yohanan b. Zaccai says: God cared for the dignity of people. An ox walks on its legs, and [so] the thief was not demeaned by carrying it on his shoulders; he [therefore] pays five [times the value]. A sheep that he carried on his shoulder he pays four [times the value], since he (i.e., the thief) was demeaned.

Rabbi Meir says: Come see how great is the value of work! An ox, whose loss causes the owner loss of work [since he is unable to plow, etc., the thief repays] fivefold. A sheep, whose loss does not cause loss of work, [the thief repays] fourfold.

3. Exodus 21:22–25

When men fight, and one of them pushes a pregnant woman and a miscarriage results, but no other damage ensues, the one responsible shall be fined according as the woman's husband may exact from him, the payment to be based on reckoning [of the age of the embryo]. But if other damage ensues [to the woman], the penalty shall be life for life, eye for eye, tooth for tooth, hand for hand, foot for foot, burn for burn, wound for wound, bruise for bruise.

4. Leviticus 5:20–26

The LORD spoke to Moses, saying: When a person sins and commits a trespass against the LORD by dealing deceitfully with his fellow in the matter of a deposit or a pledge, or through robbery, or by defrauding his fellow, or by finding something lost and lying about it; if he swears falsely regarding any one of the various things that one may do and sin thereby—when one has thus sinned and, realizing his guilt, would restore that which he got through robbery or fraud, or the deposit that was entrusted to him, or the lost thing that he found, or anything else about which he swore falsely, he shall repay the principal amount and add a fifth part to it. He shall pay it to its owner when he realizes his guilt. Then he shall bring to the priest, as his penalty to the LORD, a ram without blemish from the flock, or the equivalent, as a guilt offering. The priest shall make expiation on his behalf before the LORD, and he shall be forgiven for whatever he may have done to draw blame thereby.

5. Deuteronomy 19:16–20

If a man appears against another to testify against him maliciously and gives false testimony against him, the two parties to the dispute shall appear before the LORD, before the priests or magistrates in authority at the time, and the magistrates shall make a thorough investigation. If the man who testifies is a false witness, if he has testified falsely against his fellow, you shall do to him as he schemed to do to his fellow. Thus you will sweep out evil from your midst; others will hear and be afraid, and such evil things will not again be done in your midst.

6. Deuteronomy 25:1–3

When there is a dispute between men and they go to law, and a decision is rendered declaring the one in the right and the other in the wrong— if the guilty one is to be flogged, the magistrate shall have him lie down and be given lashes in his presence, by count, as his guilt warrants. He may be given up to forty lashes, but not more, lest being flogged further, to excess, your brother be degraded before your eyes.

7. Numbers 15:32–34

Once, when the Israelites were in the wilderness, they came upon a man gathering wood on the sabbath day. Those who found him as he was gathering wood brought him before Moses, Aaron, and the whole community. He was placed in custody, for it had not been specified what should be done to him.

8. Mishnah, *Bava Kamma* 8:1

He who injures a person is liable [for monetary compensation] on five counts: for damages, for pain, for healing, for loss of time, and for insult.

9. Babylonian Talmud, *Bava Kamma* 83b

Does the Divine Law not say "Eye for eye"? Why not take this literally to mean [putting out] the eye [of the offender]?—Let not this enter your mind, since it has been taught: You might think that where he put out his eye, the offender's eye should be put out, or where he cut off his arm, the offender's arm should be cut off, or again where he broke his leg, the offender's leg should be broken. [Not so; for] it is laid down, "He that smites any man ... And he that smites a beast ..." [Leviticus 24:20] just as in the case of smiting a beast compensation is to be paid, so also in the case of smiting a man compensation is to be paid ...

10. Maimonides (Rambam), *Mishneh Torah*, Laws of Killers and Preservation of Life 6:4

One can kill unintentionally and yet is it close to premeditated. For example, if [his action] contains something resembling unlawful behavior, or if he should have taken precautions and did not, his verdict is that he does not go to exile (i.e., the Cities of Refuge). Because his sin is severe, exile does not atone for him.

The Death Penalty
11. Genesis 9:6

Whoever sheds the blood of a man,
By man shall his blood be shed;
For in His image of God
Did God make man.

12. Exodus 21:12–17

He who fatally strikes a man shall be put to death. If he did not do it by design, but it came about by an act of God, I will assign you a place to which he can flee.

When a man schemes against another and kills him treacherously, you shall take him from My very altar to be put to death.

He who strikes his father or his mother shall be put to death.

He who kidnaps a man—whether he has sold him or is still holding him—shall be put to death.

He who insults [or "reviles"] his father or his mother shall be put to death.

13. Exodus 31:15

Six days may work be done, but on the seventh day there shall be a sabbath of complete rest, holy to the LORD; whoever does work on the sabbath day shall be put to death.

14. Leviticus 20:10–12

If a man commits adultery with a married woman, committing adultery with another man's wife, the adulterer and the adulteress shall be put to death. If a man lies with his father's wife … the two shall be put to death … If a man lies with his daughter-in-law, both of them shall be put to death …

15. Leviticus 24:17, 21

If anyone kills any human being, he shall be put to death … One who kills a beast shall make restitution for it; but one who kills a human being shall be put to death.

16. Numbers 35:30–34

If anyone kills a person, the manslayer may only be executed on the evidence of witnesses; the testimony of a single witness against a person shall not suffice for a sentence of death. You may not accept a ransom for the life of the murderer who is guilty of a capital crime; he must be put to death. Nor may you accept ransom in lieu of flight to a city of refuge, enabling one to return to live on his land before the death of the priest. You shall not pollute the land in which you live; for blood pollutes the land, and the land can have no expiation for blood that is shed on it, except by the blood of him who shed it. You shall not defile the land in which you live, in which I Myself abide, for I the LORD abide among the Israelite people.

Note: The simple reading of this source is that the City of Refuge is just that, a safe haven for one who kills unintentionally. The source in Numbers places a statute of limitations on the killer's stay there, tying it to the death of the High Priest. It is thus not clear if, according to Numbers, staying in the City of Refuge is a matter of protecting the unintentional killer, equivalent to a prison term, or a matter of atonement, as the Rabbis of the Talmud seemed to understand it. If so, this would be the closest the Jewish tradition comes to the notion of a jail term.

17. Deuteronomy 19:1–13

When the LORD your God has cut down the nations whose land the LORD your God is assigning to you, and you have dispossessed them and settled in their towns and homes, you shall set aside three cities in the land that the LORD your God is giving you to possess. You shall survey the distances, and divide into three parts the territory of the country that the LORD your God has allotted to you, so that any manslayer may have a place to flee to.—Now this is the case of the manslayer who may flee there and live: one who has killed another unwittingly, without having been his enemy in the past. For instance, a man goes with his neighbor into a grove to cut wood; as his hand swings the ax to cut down a tree, the ax-head flies off the handle and strikes the other so that he dies. That man shall flee to one of these cities and live.— Otherwise, when the distance is great, the blood-avenger, pursuing the manslayer in hot anger, may overtake him and kill him; yet he did not incur the death penalty, since he had never been the other's enemy. That is why I command you: set aside three cities. And when the LORD your God enlarges your territory, as He swore to your fathers, and gives you all the land that He promised to give your fathers—if you faithfully observe all this Instruction that I enjoin upon you this day, to love the LORD your God and to walk in His ways at all times—then you shall add three more towns to those three. Thus blood of the innocent will not be shed, bringing bloodguilt upon you in the land that the LORD your God is allotting to you. If, however, a person who is the enemy of another lies in wait for him and sets upon him and strikes him a fatal blow and then flees to one of these towns, the elders of his town shall have him brought back from there and shall hand him over to the blood-avenger to be put to death; you must show him no pity. Thus you will purge Israel of the blood of the innocent, and it will go well with you.

18. Mishnah, *Sanhedrin* 6:5

Rabbi Meir says: When a person feels sorrow, what does Shekhinah (the Divine presence) say? "My head hurts, My arm hurts." If this is the sorrow that God feels over the blood of the wicked that is shed, how much more so over the blood of the righteous!

111

19. Mishnah, *Makkot* 1:10

A Sanhedrin (a court of 23 or 71, which is authorized to try capital cases) that executes once in seven years is called "bloody"; Rabbi Elazar b. Azariah says: One in seventy years.

Rabbi Tarfon and Rabbi Akiva say: If we were on the Sanhedrin, no person would ever be executed. Rabban Shimon b. Gamaliel says: They too increase the murderers in Israel.

Contemporary Sources

Compiled by Steven Edelman-Blank and Julia Oestreich

Forms of Punishment

1. Elliot N. Dorff, "Shabbat Parashat Mi'ketz—Hanukkah 8th Day—2 Tevet 5770—Vengeance vs. Justice." Available at http://judaism. ajula.edu/Content/ContentUnit.asp?CID=905&u=8401&t=0

Part of what we generally mean by justice is retribution ... Granted that the Mishnah later made it virtually impossible to carry out the death penalty (M. Makkot 1:10) and that it transformed these modes of retribution into compensation (M. Bava Kamma 8:1), still the standard of justice is *lex talionis*, the law of fitting the punishment to the crime in an attempt to achieve an exact balance of one for the other. That, in the view of both the Torah and the Rabbis, is justice. So how is justice different from vengeance such that the former is praised and the latter condemned?

Several things mark the difference. First, justice is meted out by communal authorities—courts and/or kings in the ancient world—while the vengeance banned in Leviticus 19 is that of individuals against each other. The presumption is that the court or king will be neutral and fair in deciding whether punishment is warranted and, if so, what it should be. Judges therefore, according to Mishnaic law (M. Sanhedrin 3:4), may not be related to each other or to the accused or litigants ...

Second, justice requires that people be treated fairly—that is, that everyone be subject to the same rules. Those taking revenge, by contrast, decide by themselves what they think is appropriate to do to get even with the particular person or people from whom they are wreaking vengeance.

Finally, the agents and motives of justice and vengeance differ radically. Justice is meted out by neutral governmental authorities. Judges may be upset that they must inflict punishment on particular offenders, but if they are unrelated to them, as they should be, the judges' motivation will not be to harm particular people but rather to uphold the law so that society can live in peace.

In contrast, vengeance is inflicted by victims or their families or friends. Vengeance is therefore much more personal. As such, it can eat up the person who bears a grudge and seeks vengeance, sometimes to the point of making gaining revenge the focus of their lives.

2. **Jill Jacobs, *There Shall Be No Needy: Pursuing Social Justice through Jewish Law and Tradition* (Woodstock, VT: Jewish Lights, 2009), 195–96**

Today, roughly half of America's prisoners are incarcerated for non-violent crimes, and approximately one-fifth of prisoners are serving time for drug-related offenses. More than two-thirds of these drug offenders are serving time for low-level crimes such as possession, small-scale selling, or serving as lookouts for drug dealers. The classification of drug use as a crime, rather than as a public health issue, has resulted in the imprisonment of more than a million people at any given time; the breakup of millions of families; the loss of untold numbers of chances for treatment and rehabilitation; and an economic and social crisis occasioned by the reentry into the community each year of hundreds of thousands of former convicts, a substantial number of whom struggle with addiction, mental illness, or physical disabilities.

3. **"Reform of the Rockefeller Drug Laws," *Reform Jewish Voice of New York State*, Sept. 15, 2009. Available at http://rac.org/advocacy/rjv/issues/reform_of_the_rockefeller_drug_laws/index.cfm?**

Enacted in 1973 when Nelson Rockefeller was Governor of New York State, the Rockefeller Drug Laws require harsh prison terms for the possession or sale of relatively small amounts of drugs. The penalties apply without regard to the circumstances of the offense or the individual's character or background. Whether the person is a first-time or repeat offender, for instance, is irrelevant.

Over the course of 35 years, the Rockefeller Drug Laws have proven unjust, wasteful, and marked by racial bias. 90% of those incarcerated are African-American or Latino, despite research showing that the majority of people who use and sell drugs are white. Currently, over 13,000 individuals are incarcerated under these harsh statutes, 80% of whom have no history of violence. Confining drug offenders costs New York State over $500 million per year. There are alternative programs that are more effective in reducing crime and far less expensive than imprisonment.

4. **Sharon Brous and Daniel Sokatch, "The Possibility of Change: An Argument for Restorative Justice" in** *Righteous Indignation: A Jewish Call for Justice,* **Or N. Rose, Jo Ellen Green Kaiser, and Margie Klein, eds. (Woodstock, VT: Jewish Lights, 2008), 175–76**

Especially in the case of juvenile offenders, the system is failing at the most basic level. Rather than diverting young offenders from future criminality through rehabilitation, our juvenile justice system often serves as a university of criminality—one whose rotating door admits youthful, minor offenders and graduates them, years later, as hardened young adult criminals.

Many working for justice in both the religious and legal worlds increasingly believe a better, fairer system should be based on the model of restoration rather than retribution. Restorative justice is rooted in a recognition that the strict focus on retribution, on punishing and jailing perpetrators, fails to adequately address the deepest wounds of criminal activity, just as it fails to recognize the potential for change in people who commit crimes. Restorative justice calls for a more comprehensive response to crime, providing not only legal, but also social and spiritual mechanisms for both victims and offenders to make amends and heal.

The Death Penalty
5. **Richard A. Block, "Capital Punishment" in** *Crime and Punishment in Jewish Law: Essays and Responsa,* **Walter Jacob and Moshe Zemer, eds. (New York: Berghahn Books, 1999), 70–71**

For me, the most resonant aspect of the tradition is its reluctance to take a human life, even a life that 'deserves' to be taken, its reluctance to become a killer in response to a killing. Society certainly has the right—indeed, it has the obligation—to protect itself by punishing criminals, but it ought not kill criminals on the unproved and unprovable supposition that capital punishment saves lives by deterring crime.

Capital punishment may be just, but it cannot be administered in a just, fair and uniform manner. Our legal system is the finest humanity has ever known, but it is far from perfect. Its chief fuel is money, and its chief flaw is that only the affluent defendant can be sure of receiving an adequate defense. The history of capital punishment in western civilization in general, and in this country in particular, demonstrates that the poor, members of racial and ethnic minorities, and the physically ugly are disproportionately likely to be executed for capital crimes …

Moreover, cases in which innocent people have been wrongly convicted of capital crimes are disturbingly common. Even when there is eyewitness identification or a confession, the identification sometimes turns out to have been incorrect or the confession is revealed to have been coerced or falsified. Once a person has been executed, the injustice cannot be undone. The risk of executing innocent people cannot be eliminated so long as capital punishment is practiced.

6. **Barry D. Cytron and Earl Schwartz, *When Life is in the Balance: Life and Death Decisions in Light of the Jewish Tradition* (New York: United Synagogue of Conservative Judaism Department of Youth Activities, 1986), 191**

… the Jewish tradition's attitude toward the death penalty has been in a state of flux, too. Perhaps the current practice in Israel is instructive. For Israel is the only country where Jews alone have the privilege of taking their religious tradition, including the sources we have studied, and bringing them to life in a society.

Today, the death penalty may be invoked by Israel for only two crimes: genocide and treason during times of actual warfare.

7. **Albert Vorspan and David Saperstein, *Jewish Dimensions of Social Justice: Tough Moral Choices of Our Time* (New York: UAHC Press, 1998), 22**

The many national Jewish organizations opposed to capital punishment were shocked by the results of a number of polls showing that as many as 74 percent of all Jews *oppose* abolishing the death penalty. Jews, traditionally regarded as particularly liberal and humanitarian, voting in favor of capital punishment! What was going on?

Jews were demanding tougher measures to crack down on drug-related shootings, violence in the schools, and muggings on the streets that increased for many years until the early 1990s and, despite declining rates, remain too high. Some measure of law and order on the streets of our cities and safety in our homes had to be restored.

It is not "illiberal" to demand an end to such savagery. Like others, Jews are no longer content to articulate theories that the criminal is the product of society's failures and that reconstructing society is the surest way to reduce crime. Life and property are in jeopardy now. Daily life has become too anxiety-provoking.

Exasperated by the failure of other solutions, even Jews are tempted by politicians who exploit these anxieties. Reinstitution of the death penalty has become the vote-getting response of many politicians pandering to the public cry for law and order.

8. **Jonathan Tobin, "Questionable Sentences and False Martyrs," *Jewish World Review*, June 30, 2000**

What this debate is really about is whether or not we think it is right, or just, for the state to take the life of a person convicted of murder. Many of us simply believe it is immoral for the state to take a life, even the life of a person who has carried out a depraved and premeditated murder.

I respect that point of view, but I cannot share it.

In contrast to those who believe the death penalty undermines our respect for life, it must be pointed out that a society that prevents itself from adequately punishing murder is not a just one. No crime is a greater threat to the fabric of society than murder. We must respect the lives of the victims, not just the murderers.

9. **Progressive Jewish Alliance, Policy Statement on the Death Penalty. Available at http://www.pjalliance.org/article.aspx?ID=66&CID=9**

The capital punishment apparatus of our criminal justice system is deeply flawed. Capital defendants are often provided with inadequate legal counsel, resulting in unfair and inequitable trials. The death penalty disproportionately impacts the poor and people of color. There is no credible evidence that the death penalty deters crime. A significant danger exists that innocent people have been and will be executed because of errors in the criminal justice system.

Responses

Getting Our Priorities Right: The Call for Education, Not Incarceration[1]
Jo Hirschmann

IN RECENT years, a new urban phenomenon has emerged: city blocks that cost the government upwards of $1 million each year. These streets are dubbed "million-dollar blocks" because so many of their residents are in jail or prison that the combined cost of incarcerating them exceeds a million dollars.[2] It doesn't take much imagination to think of how these public funds could be better used. In the impoverished neighborhoods that are home to million-dollar blocks, schools, parks, environmental clean-up projects, hospitals, clinics, drug rehabilitation programs, playgrounds, and daycare centers are all in short supply or underfunded. The government has not invested adequately in these critical services, but over the past three decades, the prison system has ballooned, and taxpayers have picked up the tab. In this fiscal trade-off, the choice to fund incarceration rather than education is particularly stark.

How Did We Get Here? A Brief Look at the "War on Drugs"
The United States incarcerates a greater proportion of its people than any other country, developed or undeveloped, in the world. Between 1970 and 2007, the number of people held in state and federal prisons increased almost seven-fold.[3] However, the impact of incarceration is not spread evenly across society. Of the staggering number of incarcerated Americans (in 2007, one out of every 131 people was in jail or prison),[4] a disproportionate number of them are people of color, low-income, and/or poorly educated. Significantly, African-American men have a 22.4% chance of

1. I am grateful to Kate Rubin and Amanda Devecka-Rinear, both of whom spoke to me about their community-based work for alternatives to incarceration.
2. For more information about "million-dollar blocks," refer to the work of the Justice Mapping Center, www.justicemapping.org.
3. The Sentencing Project, "Facts about Prisons and Prisoners," July 2008. Available at http://sentencingproject.org/PublicationDetails.aspx?PublicationID=425.
4. Ibid.

being incarcerated at some point in their lives, and have only a 12.5% chance of earning a bachelor's degree.[5]

How did fiscal and policy priorities become so upended that African-American men are almost twice as likely to be incarcerated as they are to earn a college degree? To answer this, we need to understand the impact of the "war on drugs." Declared in the early 1980s, the war was a crackdown on drug-related offenses, "resulting in a record number of arrests, convictions, and sentences to prison for drug offenses."[6] Today, people incarcerated for such offenses comprise a significant proportion of all incarcerated people—25% of those in local jails, 20% in state prisons, and 55% in federal prisons.[7]

While common sense and public safety require that violent people be confined, nearly six out of ten people held in state prisons for drug offenses have no history of violence or of high-level selling activity. But, because the war on drugs considers drug use a criminal, not a social problem, the solutions do not tend to include treatment programs or any other number of social services. In fact, incarcerated people with a history of regular drug use are less than half as likely to be receiving treatment as they were in 1991.[8] This is despite the fact that repeated studies show a lower rate of recidivism among those who receive drug treatment.[9]

Not only are drug sentencing laws harsh, they are racially disparate. An oft-cited example of this is the different sentences for offenses involving crack cocaine versus powder cocaine. The two drugs have the same chemical composition, but in federal court, people caught possessing five grams of crack cocaine receive the same sentence as those caught with 500 grams of powder cocaine: a mandatory minimum of five years in prison. Partly as a result of this, on average, African-Americans serve almost as much prison time for drug offenses (58.7 months) as white people do for violent offenses (61.7 months).[10]

---

5. Hudson Link, Facts and Resouces, U.S. Prison Demographics. Available at http://hudsonlink.org/demo.shtml.
6. Marc Mauer and Ryan S. King, "A 25-Year Quagmire: The War on Drugs and Its Impact on American Society," The Sentencing Project, September 2007, 1. Available at http://sentencingproject.org/PublicationDetails.aspx?PublicationID=597.
7. Ibid., 9–10.
8. Ibid., 2.
9. Ibid., 17.
10. Ibid., 22.

The upshot is that a disproportionate number of people of color, espe-cially African-American men, are serving time in jail or prison—or will serve time in jail or prison. On America's million-dollar blocks, we find the true fiscal costs of prisons. In the neighborhoods where the least amount of funding is allocated for public services, public coffers are apparently bottomless when it comes to incarceration.

Funding Priorities: Schools or Prisons?
This reversal of funding priorities is perhaps most glaring when it comes to education. The discrepancy is apparent in at least three important ways. First, as funding for prisons has increased, funding for education has decreased. Second, schools with significant numbers of low-income students and students of color increasingly serve as a "pipeline," funneling children directly from the education system to the juvenile justice system. And third, it is much harder than it used to be for incarcerated people to access educational programs that could enhance their life chances upon release.

If we could close the discrepancy in funding, perhaps we could address these problems. We might use the principles of charitable giving that Moses Maimonides set down in Egypt in the 12th century as a guide. He understood that the highest level of *tzedakah* (charity) involves sup-porting a person before she or he falls into financial need.[11] In many ways, the discussion about incarceration in America is different from that about monetary support for the poor. But Maimonides' point is helpful because it underscores the need for systemic preventative approaches to social problems. In other words, if we correct fiscal priori-ties to emphasize education over incarceration, we could use education to improve people's chances in life, rather than using punishment as a catchall solution to deeply rooted social problems.

Under the banner of "education, not incarceration," a broad swath of advocates has identified the fiscal trade-off between schools and prisons as both a key cause and a central symptom of the over-reliance on incar-ceration. In a sobering report, the Justice Policy Institute, a think-tank that advocates for reform of adult and juvenile justice policy, puts it this way:

To be clear, [the United States] still spends more on various kinds of education than corrections … But from 1977 to 1999, total state

11. Maimonides, *Mishneh Torah, Hilkhot Matanot Aniyim* 10:7.

and local expenditures on corrections increased by 946%—about 2.5 times the rate of increase in spending on all levels of education (370%).[12]

Behind these numbers is a story in which "the impact of the decision to fund … prisons over schools has been concentrated among Americans with little education."[13] In other words, those who fail in school are most likely to end up serving time. The trade-off is dramatic and direct: in 1999, 52% of African-American male high school dropouts had prison records by their early thirties.[14]

Certainly, there is a complex string of factors leading to each individual's arrest and incarceration. However, the broader social pattern is noteworthy: those with the lowest level of education are the most likely to be incarcerated. If government used money currently spent on prisons for schools and colleges, would there be a different set of outcomes for those who currently do not even succeed in finishing high school? And if money were invested in failing schools in low-income neighborhoods, would we see an improvement in what are currently dismal graduation rates, with approximately only one-half of African-American ninth-graders graduating with their classes in four years?[15]

Many advocates argue that we must address not only the funding imbalance between schools and prisons, but also the way that some schools serve as conduits that funnel children into the correctional system. As Booth Gunter and Jamie Kizzire write,

> Across America, countless school children—particularly impoverished children of color—are being pushed out of schools and into juvenile lockups for minor misconduct that in an earlier era would have warranted counseling or a trip to the principal's office rather than a court appearance.[16]

---

12. Bruce Western, Vincent Schiraldi and Jason Ziedenberg, "Education & Incarceration," Justice Policy Institute, August 2003, 1–2. Available at http://www.justicepolicy.org/content-hmID=1811&smID=1581.htm.

13. Ibid., 5.

14. Ibid., 6.

15. NAACP Legal Defense Fund, "Dismantling the School-to-Prison Pipeline," 7. Available at http://naacpldf.org/content.aspx?article=16.

16. Booth Gunter and Jamie Kizzire, "Breaking the School-to-Prison Pipeline," Southern Poverty Law Center. Available at http://www.alternet.org/story/75533/.

Even though youth violence is decreasing, schools are taking a "zero-tolerance" approach to discipline.[17] According to the New York Civil Liberties Union (NYCLU), this involves using "suspension, expulsion, citations, arrest, and juvenile and criminal charges to deal with often minor disciplinary problems."[18]

This approach comes with grave consequences. According to the NYCLU, "a child who has been suspended is more likely to be retained in grade, to drop out, to commit a crime, and/or to end up incarcerated as an adult." The students targeted for "zero-tolerance" discipline policies are disproportionately African-American and Latino, and they have learning disabilities at a far higher rate than that of the overall student population.[19] Many of them never return to school, creating a costly set of long-term social problems that could potentially be avoided with investment on the front-end in quality schools. If children at schools in low-income neighborhoods had access to the same resources that their peers in wealthy communities have, they too might possess the tools necessary to succeed in school. As it is, however, those who have the hardest time in school are the most likely to end up in education's better-funded counterpart: the penal system.

Learning Behind Bars: The Transformative Power of Education
Lawmakers are enthusiastic about funding and expanding the criminal justice system, but the programs receiving that support are both costly and ineffective. Recidivism rates are high: 68% of former prisoners are rearrested for a new offense within three years of release, and 52% are sent back to prison for a new offense or parole violation.[20] However, a string of studies shows that taking college classes while in prison reduces a person's chance of reoffending. Despite this, it is much harder for convicts to pursue this type of study now than it was 15 years ago. Between 1970 and 1994, prisoners could receive federal tuition assistance, and there were 350 college programs in prisons in 45 states. But in 1994, President Clinton signed

---

17. Ibid., 2.
18. New York Civil Liberties Union, "Fact Sheet: School to Prison Pipeline," 2007. Available at http://www.nyclu.org/news_and_resources/allpublications.
19. Ibid.
20. Hudson Link for Higher Education in Prison, Facts and Resources, Re-entry and Recidivism. Available at http://hudsonlink.org/reentry.shtml.

the Violent Crime Control and Law Enforcement Act, making prisoners ineligible for this financial assistance. Across the country, the number of prison college programs dropped to less than 10.[21]

For the past decade, teachers from Hudson Link, an organization based in Ossining, NY, have taught inmates at Sing Sing Prison, with dramatically positive results. During this time, 138 prisoners earned a bachelor's degree through Hudson Link's programs—and not one of them has returned to prison. As one former student, who is now a teacher with the program says, "Hudson Link is rooted in a vision of the humanity of all people, of the potential of all people ... Other people, chance, providence threw me a lifeline ... that fertilized another part of me."[22] Belatedly, and without anything close to adequate funding, prison college programs repair a small part of the damage done by an approach that favors incarceration over education, punishment over rehabilitation.

Education is transformative, as Jewish tradition and culture repeatedly remind us. Whether secular or religious in nature, education enriches our lives, opens doors, and connects us to worlds beyond ourselves. This is true in a *beit midrash* (traditional Jewish house of study), in an elementary school classroom, and in a prison cell. It is true in an affluent suburb and it is true on a million-dollar block. Education is transformative in all these places, but it is most effective when it is properly resourced and when it is treated as the top priority, not as a last resort. This means that, instead of being the loser in the fiscal competition with incarceration, education must become the winner—a change that would truly allow transformative educational opportunities to flourish in every community.

---

21. "The Impact of College Study in Prison," *Clarion: Newspaper of the Professional Staff Congress/ City University of New York*, November 2008, 6.
22. Interview with Gregory Frederick, New York City, December 30, 2008.

Reading the Rabbis in Their Own World: Contextualizing Rabbinic Views of Capital Punishment

Mark Ankcorn

Understanding Rabbinic Sources on Capital Punishment

WHEN I was a young prosecutor, one of the defense attorneys whom I had faced in several trials used to ask prospective jurors during the *voir dire* process a question that I thought was odd. "If you were sitting here at this table, Mrs. Smith," he would inquire, "would you want a person like you on the jury deciding your fate?" His point, if he had one, was to test how unbiased the potential juror really was. Was he or she enough of an impartial and reasonable person to listen to the law and the facts and decide a case on its merits, or not? He stopped asking the question when an older male juror replied, "Hell, no! If I were on trial, I'd want my brother and my mother and the rest of my family on that jury. People who would vote 'not guilty' no matter what the evidence was!"

This is what we forget when we consider the rabbinic sources on capital punishment. The Rabbis were not pondering the ethical and normative design of a model penal system, to be enacted into law by a representative legislature and administered by an adversarial system where each person accused would be entitled to a free attorney and enjoy the right to remain silent when arrested. The Rabbis lived and worked and taught as a distinct and frequently oppressed minority, where teaching Torah was sometimes considered a capital offense and punishment was imposed by brutal and capricious despots. We cannot forget that they were creating rules for the Jewish community to use when it decided on the fate of its own people—that is to say, when sitting in judgment of their brothers and sons and cousins.

With the possible exception of Spain in the 12th and 13th centuries, the imposition of capital punishment by a Jewish court likely never happened. The governors and magistrates appointed by the Roman emperors, the Byzantine rulers, the kings and dukes of Western Europe, and the czars and barons of Eastern Europe never permitted serious crimes to be judged by the Jews as an internal problem. Certainly none would have abdicated their authority over a murder or a sexual assault.

Indeed, recognition of Jews' minority status is itself part of Jewish law. A key principle of *halakhah* is that in civil and criminal matters, *dina d'malkhuta dina*, "the law of the sovereign [the state] is the law." Thus, throughout time, when the non-Jewish authority of a particular state created a rule backed up by force, that rule trumped whatever the Torah required and in fact became part of the legal system of the Jewish community in that state. For example, if a secular court declared that a Jew was contractually obligated to pay a sum of money, then the Jewish courts would require the debt to be paid, even if Jewish law would have yielded a different result. The Rabbis clearly knew the limits of their own authority. They also knew the harsh consequences for the entire community if the sovereign (the one with the soldiers and the weapons) felt that his power was being diminished or flouted.

Small wonder, then, that the Rabbis consistently sought out whatever slim justification would support a "not guilty" verdict when sitting in judgment of other Jews. In a world where life was cheap and Jewish lives considered of virtually no worth whatsoever, it is even less surprising that Jews were extremely reluctant to seek death as a means to punish other Jews.

Even a casual reader of the Torah, however, would discover that Jewish tradition considered capital punishment to be an unremarkable part of the Jewish justice system. The death penalty was prescribed for a whole range of offenses that would seem to us to be fairly petty crimes, or hardly criminal at all. In Numbers 15:32–35, for instance, God tells Moses to stone to death a man who was discovered gathering wood on Shabbat. Certainly, though, the untimely clearing of brush is not considered a criminal offense, capital or otherwise, in any state that I have ever heard of. For a civilization that so highly values life, this carelessness with capital punishment stands out at best as an anachronism, and at worst as a moral failing that calls into question the compassion and love of the divine author of Jewish law.

The Rabbis apparently agreed with that assessment and went to considerable lengths to read capital punishment out of the Torah. They parsed the verses with precision to restrict capital punishment to rare cases. For example, they defined the "disloyal and defiant" son who was to be publicly put to death as required by Deuteronomy 21:21, as being a male who was disobedient after eating gluttonously from partially cooked meat and making himself drunk on partially diluted wine. Even then, he was still only considered a "disloyal and defiant" son if he had eaten the meat and gotten drunk in the first three months after turning 13 years of age, and only if the wine and meat were purchased cheaply with stolen money—and so forth. The requirements that the Rabbis constructed from their careful reading of just a few verses in the Torah lead them to conclude that there never was, nor would there ever be, a situation in which a "disloyal and defiant" son could be lawfully executed.

The early Rabbis did not see themselves as being empowered to change the substantive law. To them, the Torah was God-given and of unquestionable authority, defining offenses and setting their punishments. But the Rabbis could and did alter procedural requirements to tilt the playing field sharply against the imposition of capital punishment. In the oft-quoted formulation from the Mishnah from *Makkot* 1:10, if a court imposed more than one death sentence in seven years, it was considered murderous. Another Rabbi responded that if a court imposed more than one such sentence in 70 years, it was to be considered murderous. Rabbi Akiva and his colleague Rabbi Tarfon, both giants of the early Rabbinic era, then stated that had they been members of the court, no defendant would ever have been executed.

And yet, the last word in this Mishnah was given to Rabbi Shimon ben Gamliel, who became the president of the Sanhedrin (the rabbinic high court) and was a key figure in the formation of post-Temple Judaism. He said of Rabbi Akiva and Rabbi Tarfon that "they too increase the murderers in Israel." With that, the Mishnah turned its attention to other matters, leaving later generations to draw their own conclusions about a question that was not practical, but entirely academic, given the lack of a properly constituted rabbinic court sitting in session on the steps of a functioning "Third Temple" in Jerusalem. According to Jewish tradition, only such a court could properly render a capital verdict.

Applying the Rabbinic Tradition to Our Times
Where does this leave us as Jews in considering the appropriate moral stance toward our modern, secular criminal justice system? Given the historical reality of the Rabbis' world, which was vastly different from our own, should we let their extreme and compassionate aversion to taking Jewish life stop us from supporting a criminal justice system that includes the imposition of capital punishment?

125

The Mishnah gave the last word to Rabbi Shimon ben Gamliel because without discipline and rigor, compassion is meaningless—just as rigor without compassion is cruel. "The murderers in Israel" would have increased without the imposition of the death penalty, which suggests to us that easy pronouncements of charity and mercy make us feel good but have deleterious consequences in the long run. A justice system that always bends toward compassion will never have the steel required to keep bad people in check, nor to show what true justice looks like in practice. More than that, the necessity for capital punishment renders all of our moralizing about human dignity mere rhetoric that makes us feel good about our "ethical stand" when it carries no personal cost.

Treating everyone like a member of the human family sounds nice, but in practice it is horrible. A husband who treats every woman in the world just like his wife has no credibility when he professes his affection for the one woman to whom he is married. When your child looks up at you adoringly and says, "I love you," your heart soars and you feel fulfilled in ways that nothing else can make you feel. That gets tarnished some, though, when your child then tells his stuffed bear that he loves it most of all. Love, to be meaningful, must be limited and measured; so too with compassion and justice. We cannot demonstrate the same mercy toward those who kill as we do to those who don't.

Ernest van den Haag, the late professor of jurisprudence at Fordham University, posited this hypothetical situation: suppose that we made murders committed on Mondays, Wednesdays, and Fridays punishable by life sentences, and murders committed on all other days punishable by the death penalty. Does anyone truly believe that the murder rate on Mondays, Wednesdays, and Fridays would remain unchanged? If you doubt that career criminals are thoughtful enough to adjust their behavior to the law, ask prosecutors and police in Nevada, Arizona, and Oregon what happened after California passed its harsh Three Strikes law in the mid-1990s. The law mandated a life sentence for anyone convicted of a felony who already had two prior serious felony offenses on their record. Parole officials in California still talk of the mass criminal exodus from their state in the wake of the law's enactment. Clearly, sentencing schemes have value as a deterrent, and that is all the more true for capital punishment, which is the ultimate sentence.

Capital punishment also makes an important moral statement about our priorities as a society. It says that there are some things that a person can do that are truly beyond redemption and that society cannot forgive. It says that life matters and those who show depraved disregard for their fellow human beings will not be permitted to exist in our society.

This is the position ultimately taken after considerable debate by the State of Israel, which administers capital punishment only for the crime of genocide. In its 60-year history, Israel has executed only one person— Adolph Eichmann, the architect of the Nazi death camps—and only then after a public trial at which he was represented by a team of attorneys. The Jewish people in that moment showed far more humanity toward Eichmann than he ever did toward the millions of Jews he slaughtered. Yet, without the ultimate verdict of guilt in the face of overwhelming evidence, and the resulting death sentence, that display of humanity would have been a farce, a shallow expression of weakness and immorality that would have haunted us for centuries. It would have communicated that Jewish lives are cheap and unimportant, even to other Jews.

That is why Israel's failure to execute the assassin of its Prime Minister Yitzhak Rabin continues to mock that society. A calculated political actor in full command of his faculties—the son of a rabbi and a law student at the time of the shooting, who had twice before attempted the assassination—Rabin's murderer, Yigal Amir, sits in prison to this day. He married a woman and fathered a child with her while in prison, and was even able to attend his son's *bris*.

This is not nearly the only such case of murderers having the last laugh over their victims from prison, unrepentant and unremorseful. No wonder Americans are intensely cynical about the workings of the criminal justice system. *The Washington Post* has reported that only 4% of Americans believe that a life sentence really means that convicted murders will spend the rest of their days in prison. On average, people think that a convicted murderer sentenced to a life term will be released after only eight or ten years in custody. But given these attitudes about what it really means to be punished for committing a crime, it is all the more important for our society to have an emphatic stance that those who commit heinous murders must pay the ultimate price.

Our communal reluctance to impose the death penalty on our own people is understandable, for a host of historical and sociological reasons. We err, however, when we lavish love and compassion on those who don't deserve it, treating everyone as if he or she were a family member or friend, ultimately deserving of forgiveness for all bad acts. It is an insult to those we truly do love and serves only to encourage the very violence we profess to abhor. Capital punishment needs to be part of any judicial system that takes human life seriously. Supporting the death penalty is not only in keeping with our Jewish moral framework, but it is also compelled by our serious commitment to preserving life and doing justice for everyone, including victims.

The Role of Punishment and the Death Penalty
Laurie L. Levenson

The Goals of Punishment

CLASSICALLY, THE meting out of punishment in American criminal law is based upon four purposes: retribution, deterrence, incapacitation, and rehabilitation. Not all of these rationales work in every case, but they are the building blocks of criminal law. A simple example will demonstrate how these purposes of punishment are used in sentencing a defendant to prison.

1. *Retribution*. Imagine a bank robber is charged with threatening a teller with his gun and taking $500 from a bank. He is apprehended and convicted. Why put him in prison?

First, we punish him because he broke the rules. In its simplest sense, retribution is encapsulated in the phrase, "You did the crime, now you must do the time." In other words, the defendant "deserves" to be punished because he violated society's laws. By punishing the defendant, we reaffirm society's values.

While retribution is a key theory of punishment, there are problems with it, just as there are with the other theories behind punishment. At its essence, it is a theory based on the need for vengeance. Even if the defendant promises not to commit any other offenses, and we are confident that he will not, we still punish him because he owes a debt to society. Retribution, as a theory, thus assumes that all of society's laws are fair and that, morally, the defendant deserves to be punished.

However, what if the bank robber committed the crime because he needed the money to buy food for his children? Are we confident enough in the fairness of society's laws to claim that the defendant deserves to be punished because of his actions? There are many inequities in our society and we are always at risk of punishing people for violating rules they had no say in creating.

Additionally, retribution assumes that the defendant can "pay society back" for his crime by being incarcerated. Sending our bank robber to prison will not reimburse the bank for his crime. Neither will capital punishment bring a murder victim back to life or make the victim's family whole again. The Torah's insistence on an "eye for eye, tooth for tooth" and "life for life"[1] is a reminder that punishment should be proportional, but it is folly to believe that punishment will make a victim whole.

Finally, there are practical reasons why retribution is problematic. America has been on a crusade to incarcerate criminal offenders. Right now, there are over 2.3 million Americans in prison.[2] The United States has less than 5% of the world's population, but almost a quarter of the world's prisons. China, which is four times more populous than the United States, is a distant second, with 1.6 million of its people in prison.[3] The cost of incarcerating America's defendants in state and federal prisons is more than $60 billion.[4] Even if we believed that it is appropriate to punish every person for his or her misconduct, the reality is that we cannot afford to do so.

2. *Deterrence.* But let's get back to our bank robber. Another reason we might want to incarcerate him is to set an example for others; deterrence, in other words. Using a cost-benefit analysis,[5] the legal system assumes that our robber can be stopped from committing future bank robberies if we make the punishment for robbery greater than the benefits. Moreover, not only will he be deterred, but so will others who know of his punishment because they too will perform the same cost-benefit analysis and realize that robbery is not worth it.

The flaws in this deterrence theory should be apparent. First, it assumes that criminals are rational, calculating actors. Under this model, before a would-be bank robber violates the law, he will pause, think about the consequences of his actions, realize that he will get caught, and decline to commit the crime. The reality is that bank robbers, like most defendants, do not engage in such rational, calculated decision making before they commit crimes. More often than not, people commit crimes because

---

1. Exodus 21:23–27.
2. Report of Pew Center on the States (Feb. 28, 2008). Available at http://www.pewcenteronthestates.org.
3. Adam Liptak, "America Tops Global Count of Prison Inmates," *International Herald Tribune*, April 24, 2008.
4. U.S. Department of Justice, Bureau of Justice Statistics (2005), "Direct expenditure for each of the major criminal justice functions." Available at http://www.ojp.usdoj.gov/bjs/glance/exptyp.htm.
5. See Jeremy Bentham, *Principles of Penal Law*, Pt. II, bk. 1, ch. 3 in *Works of Jeremy Bentham*, J. Bowring, ed. (1843), 396, 402.

of addiction, mental compulsion, emotional outbursts, or desperation. They do not carefully calculate the costs and benefits of their actions.

Moreover, even if they did, uncertainty as to their chances of being captured and the severity of their punishment might make them discount any potential consequences. Perhaps there are some white-collar criminals who carefully think about the benefits and costs of committing crimes (although in my experience, they don't, because their greed has become an addiction), but most defendants commit crimes because they are driven to do so. The proof that deterrence does not really work is that the recidivism rate in some states is as high as 67% for defendants—having been punished for one crime, they are paroled and commit another.[6]

The second flaw in the deterrence theory is that it assumes that criminals don't want to go to prison and that we know how much incarceration is needed to deter someone from committing a crime. Punishment is not an exact science. How much time in prison will deter a kid with no future job or educational opportunities from taking his chances by selling drugs that would net him hundreds of thousands of dollars? What if that kid thinks it is cool to go to prison because his father, grandfather, brothers, or friends are there? Deterrence works for people who are already reluctant to commit crime and don't want to go to prison. For those who see prison as a badge of honor, it may have the opposite effect.

Finally, there are ethical objections to punishing someone in order to affect other people's behavior. If we really wanted to deter people, we could impose draconian sentences on celebrities, so that others will not want to be in their situation. What if we flogged pop singer Britney Spears on national television as punishment for a parking ticket? Sure, it might deter other scofflaws, but such punishment would be wrong. Famous philosophers, including Immanuel Kant, have long argued that it is immoral to punish someone solely to influence the actions of others.[7]

3. *Incapacitation.* A third reason for punishing our bank robber might be to take him out of society and prevent him, at least for the period he is in prison, from committing more crimes. But prisoners commit crimes in prison all the time! Incarceration cannot and does not prevent defen-

---

6. U.S. Department of Justice, Bureau of Justice Statistics (2005), Criminal Offender Statistics, Summary Findings. Available at http://www.ojp.usdoj.gov.
7. Immanuel Kant, *The Philosophy of Law*, W. Hastie, trans. (Edinburgh, 1887).

dants from committing crimes. I have prosecuted murders, drug trafficking, and frauds that were committed by people already behind bars.

Incapacitation, as a theory of punishment, assumes that we have the resources and the skills to prevent defendants from committing crimes in prison. It also assumes that these defendants will never reenter society, where they could continue to commit crimes. Neither of these assumptions is true. It simply won't work to lock everyone up; at some point, given limited resources, they will be released and will continue to commit crimes.

4. *Rehabilitation.* Finally, some might argue that our bank robber needs to go to prison so that he can be rehabilitated. Given the realities of today's prisons, such thinking is pure foolishness. Inmates don't get "better" in prison. If anything, they tend to become better criminals. We are unwilling to invest the resources necessary to give inmates programs that will educate and reform them.

Moreover, it is unclear whether people can change those characteristics that make them prone to commit crime. For example, many experts believe that the moral makeup of a person is determined at a very early age and that very little can be done after that to change those basic characteristics. Even if such change were theoretically possible, exactly how do you teach someone who has already committed murder or robbery that it is not right to kill or rob?

Thus, while there are theories of punishment, they are flawed at best and won't necessarily work for our bank robber or for many other criminals. So where does that leave us? Do we just throw up our hands and never punish a criminal? Clearly, abandoning our justice system is not the answer. However, it probably makes sense to consider alternative approaches to dealing with crime.

Other Responses to Crime

In my experience, the best approach is preventing crime in the first place. To do this, we need to understand the causes of crime. Some defendants commit crimes because they have evil inclinations. Most, however, commit crimes for other reasons. Sometimes, it is because they come from a family background or culture where society's rules are not respected. They have been treated as the "other" and do not feel that they are party to the social contract. Other defendants commit crimes because they lack the education or opportunity to choose another course. If you are a kid growing up in poverty and society basically expects you to fail, it takes a lot of fortitude and good luck to avoid the criminal justice system. We must focus on children, improving education, and expanding opportunity. Improving the overall quality of our society won't save everyone, but it is bound to have a positive impact on the criminal justice system overall.

Some people have suggested that we look to other models of justice, such as "restorative justice" programs, to improve the criminal justice system. In restorative justice programs, the perpetrator meets directly with the victim to make amends for his or her crime and pledges to follow a new course. Frankly, I am not at all confident that such programs work, except for a narrow category of non-violent, petty criminals. For restorative justice programs to be successful, both the perpetrator and the victim have to trust each other, but trust does not come naturally in these situations. It also requires a tremendous amount of human resources, but the lack of such resources has undermined these programs. Finally, it is not at all clear that people have the emotional tools needed to make restorative justice work. *Teshuvah* (repentance) is a great ideal, but is rarely achieved through the criminal justice system.

Where does that leave us? Probably the most honest answer is that it leaves us in a quandary. The American criminal justice system is a dumping ground, our answer to most of society's ills. For instance, by some estimates, as many as 300,000 men and women in American jails and prisons suffer from serious mental disorders.[8] In some states, the number of prisoners with mental illness is doubling every 10 years.[9] Also, up to 75% of inmates used alcohol or drugs at the time they committed their crimes,[10] and over 50% of the women in our prisons report that

---

8. Jamie Fellner, "Pro Se Litigation Ten Years After AEDPA: A Corrections Quandary: Mental Illness and Prison Rules," 41 *Harvard Civil Rights-Civil Liberties Law Review* (Summer 2006), 391, 392.

9. Sasha Abramsky & Jamie Fellner, *Ill Equipped: U.S. Prisons and Offenders with Mental Illness* 19 (2003), Human Rights Watch. Available at http://www.hrw.org/reports/2003/usa1003/usa1003.pdf.

10. U.S. Department of Justice, Bureau of Justice Statistics (2008), Criminal Offender Statistics, Summary Findings. Available at http://www.ojp.usdoj.gov/bjs/crimoff.htm #inmates.pdf.

they have been sexually or physically abused.[11] Nearly 50% of all inmates come from families in which other members are incarcerated.[12]

These statistics indicate that we dump people into the criminal justice system rather than addressing their needs. Substantial cutbacks in our mental health system have poured many mentally ill people into the streets and then funneled them through the revolving door of our jails. The role of prisons and juvenile detention centers should not be to house the rejects of our society. There is no natural lobby for many of these people, and the lobbies that do exist—such as powerful prison guard unions—favor the status quo. We even create "wars" on drugs that provide financial and political incentives for law enforcement and military institutions to maintain the status quo. And in lieu of creating real immigration policies, we increase our efforts to prosecute illegal aliens.

If punishment is to serve as a means of teaching people a lesson, deterring their misbehavior, and making victims whole, then changes are desperately needed. The best approach I have seen is the model used in many new drug courts in our country. It starts with picking the right people for the job. Police officers, prosecutors, and judges will have to work hand-in-hand with social service workers. They will have to get society to invest resources in order to enable them to form individual connections with the parties in their cases. This will end the cycle of processing criminal defendants and victims as if they were sausage meat going through a machine, and will make our treatment of them more humane.

The heart of the criminal justice system is, after all, people—not numbers, not dollars, not statistics. Once that basic truth is appreciated, the role of punishment is likely to be more productive.

The Death Penalty

As difficult as it is to determine the role of punishment in contemporary culture, it's even harder to determine what punishments are appropriate for certain crimes. The ultimate example of this is the controversy over when the death penalty might be appropriate, if at all.

For almost a decade, I served as a federal prosecutor. I tried murder cases and witnessed the unspeakable things people do to each other.

---

11. U.S. Department of Justice, Bureau of Justice Statistics (2008), Criminal Offender Statistics, Summary Findings. Available at http://www.ojp.usdoj.gov/bjs/crimoff.htm #inmates.pdf.
12. Ibid.

I struggled daily with how we can protect and sanctify life. Yet, I am relieved that I never had to play God; I never had to seek the death penalty. It was the one decision I never wanted to make. Even as a hardened prosecutor, I found it difficult to support the death penalty. There are just too many problems with it.

By and large, I believe the death penalty to be a hoax on the American public. There is no credible evidence that it serves as a deterrent. In fact, ample anecdotal evidence suggests that the notoriety of being a capital killer has actually prompted some people to commit heinous crimes. Perhaps the most notable story involves an inmate who obtained his early release from prison by helping to perfect the electric chair.[13] No sooner was he paroled than he committed a murder that promptly landed him in his own invention. Certainly, the death penalty did not serve as a deterrent for him. Even though he was intimately familiar with the punishment he would receive, he still committed the crime.

The death penalty is also a hoax because we have not developed a set of trial and appellate procedures to ensure that only the guilty will be condemned. Recent DNA testing has shown the alarming frequency with which innocent persons have been wrongfully convicted. There have been 223 post-conviction exonerations in the United States due to DNA evidence.[14] In Illinois, a moratorium on the death penalty was finally imposed when more defendants on death row were being exonerated than were being executed. A 50% error rate is unacceptable in any endeavor, let alone in those involving life and death.

In order to prevent errors, the courts have adopted procedures designed to ensure fair and accurate trials. However, even with these procedures, wrongful convictions continue to occur, and DNA exonerations are probably just the tip of the iceberg. Most murder cases are not built with DNA evidence. Rather, they rely on eyewitness identifications, informants, and confessions, all notoriously unreliable.

Interestingly, American law allows the introduction of types of evidence Jewish law would reject. For example, American courts have allowed death

---

13. Edmund G. (Pat) Brown and Dick Adler, *Public Justice, Private Mercy: A Governor's Education on Death Row* (New York: Weidenfeld & Nicholson, 1989).
14. See Innocence Project at http://www.innocenceproject.org/content351.php; Death Penalty Information Center at http://www.deathpenaltyinfo.org/innocence-and-death-penalty #in-yr-rc.

penalty convictions that were based partially upon false confessions or informant testimony. Under Jewish law, the testimony of an informant is barred. Ironically, Maimonides held that informers themselves should be put to death.[15] Indeed, in approximately 25% of DNA exoneration cases, innocent defendants had made incriminating statements, falsely confessed to the crime, or pled guilty.[16] Yet, confessions are not admissible evidence in Jewish law because, as the Talmud states, "no man may call himself a wrongdoer."[17] False confessions plague our criminal justice system and put the most vulnerable defendants, juveniles and mentally deficient defendants, at greatest risk of being executed for crimes they did not commit or did not understand the implications of.

Moreover, the American procedures for handling death penalty cases almost guarantee that neither the defense nor the prosecution will be happy with the case's outcome. For example, it is not unusual for there to be a 15- to 20-year delay between the commission of a crime and the convict's execution. In fact, a death penalty inmate is much more likely to die of natural causes than to be executed. Currently in California, more than 30 people have been sitting on death row for over 25 years, 119 have been sitting there for over 20 years, and 240 have been sitting there for over 15 years.[18] Part of the reason for this delay has been the dearth of lawyers who are willing and competent to handle these cases. More than 50% of California's death row inmates do not have counsel. When these procedural realities were added to the fact that the death penalty has been applied in a discriminatory manner, former Supreme Court Justice Harry Blackmun proclaimed that he would "no longer attempt to tinker with the machinery of death."[19] Justice Blackmun ultimately favored

---

15. Maimonides, *Mishneh Torah, Hovel u-Mazzik* 8:10–11.
16. There are many reasons a suspect may confess to a crime he or she did not commit. Sometimes, the suspect is coerced during interrogation. Other times, the defendant who falsely confesses is vulnerable to suggestion because of youth or limited mental capacity. To understand more about false confessions, see The Innocence Project, "Understand the Causes of False Confessions" (2008). Available at http://www.innocenceproject.org/ understand/False-Confessions.php.
17. Babylonian Talmud, *Sanhedrin* 9b.
18. Judge Arthur L. Alarcon, "Remedies for California's Death Row Deadlock," 80 *Southern California Law Review* 697 (2007).
19. *Callins v. Collins*, 510 U.S. 1141, 1145 (1994) (Blackmun, J., dissenting).

abandoning the death penalty because there is no way to ensure that it is used in a fair and appropriate manner.

Problems in Applying the Death Penalty

It is inaccurate to claim that the death penalty represents the Torah prescription of an "eye for eye, tooth for tooth" and "life for life."[20] The truth is that the death penalty is imposed in such an arbitrary manner that there is no guarantee that it will be imposed only on those who actually deserve it. Prosecutors have enormous discretion. Defendants who have committed heinous killings may receive reduced sentences because their testimony is needed against co-defendants. However, the two biggest factors at play in deciding who will be subject to the death penalty are geographic location and race.

In some large jurisdictions, there are so many killings that a number of those who kill in a manner that would result in the death penalty elsewhere do not end up facing the death penalty. On the other hand, small, rural jurisdictions are notorious for being particularly aggressive in seeking the death penalty. A defendant who robs and kills a convenience store owner may face the death penalty in one town and only a life sentence in another.

However, race is the biggest elephant in the room. Although the Supreme Court has refused to strike down the death penalty as discriminatory per se, it has repeatedly recognized that racism pervades the criminal justice system.[21] Studies show that a person who kills a white victim is almost four times more likely to receive the death penalty than a person who kills

---

20. Exodus 21:23–27. Interestingly, Rabbinic literature (for example, the Talmud, *Bava Kamma* 83b-84a) deals with this verse in a complex way. Several opinions suggest that "eye for eye" should not be read literally, but rather that the Torah intended to teach that one should pay punitive damages for injuries.
21. There are many ways this racism is evidenced in the criminal justice system. First, there are a disproportionate number of people of color who are criminal defendants. For example, although Black Americans make up only 12.7% of the U.S. population, they make up 48.2% of all adults in prisons and jails. Second, people of color tend to be targeted by law enforcement. Because of racial profiling, Blacks and Hispanics are substantially more likely to be stopped by the police. For more information regarding racism in the criminal justice system, see "Factsheet: How is the Criminal Justice System Racist?" *Defending Justice: An Activist Resource Kit*, Public Research Associates (2005). Available at http://www.publiceye.org/defendingjustice/pdfs/factsheets/10-Fact%20Sheet%20-%20System%20as%20Racist.pdf.

a non-white victim. At least 55% of inmates currently sitting on death row are minorities.[22] More subtle racism also influences the system. Nearly every year, the Supreme Court decides a case in which prosecutors have intentionally sought to dismiss minorities from juries in death penalty cases in an attempt to keep away potentially sympathetic jurors. Thus, the death penalty is not applied on an even playing field. If a minority defendant is on trial, the field is tilted toward a capital verdict.

The death penalty is also a very expensive proposition. The cost of keeping an inmate incarcerated for life is significantly less than that of prosecuting a capital case through the appellate process. Capital defendants are entitled to two sets of everything—two sets of lawyers, two stages of a trial (the guilty phase and the penalty phase), and two sets of appeals (direct appeals and habeas corpus proceedings). If voters just voted based on their pocketbooks, they would outlaw the death penalty tomorrow.

Because of these necessary procedural guarantees, some jurisdictions have tried to contain costs by paying capital defense lawyers rock bottom salaries. For example, in Alabama, a lawyer handling a death penalty case is paid less than $2,000 to investigate and prepare a capital case, including the preparation of a post-conviction appeal. If the lawyer spends a minimum of 500 hours on the capital case, he or she then earns $4 per hour.[23] As they say, "You get what you pay for." Unfortunately, this means that poor defendants are much more likely to receive the death penalty just because they do not have the resources to defend their case.

Finally, in addition to concerns over procedure and fairness, there are questions as to whether the death penalty is justified by a need to "bring closure" to the victims' families. The drawn-out process of death penalty appeals frustrates many victims' families and makes it nearly impossible for them to experience closure. Moreover, these families frequently express a preference for having the defendant serve life in prison rather than be executed. They do not want the execution on their conscience,

22. Death Penalty Information Center, "Facts About Death Penalty," Oct. 15, 2008. Available at http://www.deathpenaltyinfo.org.
23. Stephen B. Bright, *The Death Penalty: Casualties and Costs of the War on Crime*, The City Club of Cleveland, Cleveland, OH, Nov. 1997. Speech.

or they actually see the execution as being the "easy way out" for the defendant. They would much prefer if the defendant spent years rotting behind bars.

On the international front, the use of the death penalty in the United States stands out like a sore thumb. Only countries like Iraq, Iran, and China still use the death penalty. Countries cannot join the European Union unless they renounce it as an option for punishment, and the International Court of Justice does not employ it. The United States is in a distinct minority by using capital punishment, which it applies not only to intentional killings, but even to felony-murder cases in which a victim's killing might be accidental.

The United States Supreme Court has slowly chipped away at the scope of the death penalty, however. In the last 10 years, it has held that it is unconstitutional to impose capital punishment on minors and the mentally retarded, and to seek the death penalty for non-homicide crimes, including child rape. "Evolving standards of decency" have led to a trend that increasingly rejects the death penalty as a punishment. It is, therefore, not surprising that 16 states have abandoned it.[24] And, with the exception of jurors in Texas and Florida, there is a growing reluctance to impose it as a punishment, even in notorious cases.[25] For example, Zacarias Moussaoui, the alleged "20th hijacker" in the 9/11 attack, was not sentenced to death in his jury trial.

Conclusion

Yet, the practice of capital punishment survives. The frontline in the fight against the death penalty is now focused on whether there is a constitutional manner of execution. We have come to realize that there is no nice way to kill someone. For now, lethal injection is legally acceptable, but even challenges to that practice continue. This leads us back to the basic question: Should the death penalty be abolished? Generally, I would say yes. But I hesitate. I sincerely believe that killing is wrong, and if it is wrong for the defendant, it is also wrong for the state. Yet, I am also honest enough to admit that there could be a case—something so heinous, so barbaric, and so unforgivable—that I would consider making

24. Ibid.
25. Adam Feuer, "Aversion to Death Penalty, but No Lack of Cases," *The New York Times*, Mar. 10, 2008.

an exception. The only example that comes to mind is that of a homicidal maniac like Adolph Eichmann. His butchery and evil was so colossal that Israel seems to have been justified in imposing the ultimate punishment upon him, the only time in the history of the State that it has done so.

I wish I didn't have this exception in mind. I wish I could be the absolutist who says that I could never support the death penalty. I wish the Torah made it much easier on us with an absolute prohibition of, "You shall not murder."[26] But it doesn't. Instead, it provides that sometimes capital punishment is warranted. Why does it do this? Perhaps for the very reason that I leave open the possibility of the exception. Playing God isn't all we are doing when we decide whether or not to maintain the death penalty as a punishment in our society. We are also trying to decide how best to preserve human life overall. Exceptions to our opinions on this issue remind us that life and death matters are never easy. The law does not have answers to all of our questions. The important thing is that we keep struggling with this question: what kind of punishment will protect and preserve the overall sanctity of human life?

---

26. Exodus 20:13.

Conclusion: The Ethics of Social Justice

W E HOPE that this volume has demonstrated, beyond any doubt, that compassion for others is a Jewish value. This value comes out of the commandment, "Love your fellow as yourself" (Lev. 19:18), which is a manifestation of the core Jewish belief that each of us is created in the image of God (Gen. 1:27 and 5:1). As such, we must preserve not only the life and the health of others, but their dignity as well.

Some of the ways that we are obliged to do this are straightforward. For instance, we must take care of people in our society who are poor, abandoned, or sick. Even so, as we have seen in the discussion of Case 1, carrying out this duty is not always as simple as one might hope or expect. Because everyone has a limited amount of time, energy, and resources, we must make choices about whom to help and how to help them. There are, as we have seen, a number of different ways to approach this dilemma.

Yet, Jews are obliged not only to take care of others, but also to treat them fairly. The Torah commands:

> When a stranger resides with you in your land, you shall not wrong him. The stranger who resides with you shall be to you as one of your citizens; you shall love him as yourself, for you were strangers in the land of Egypt: I the Lord am your God (Lev. 19:33–34).

Case 2 raises many questions about how to live out this idea today, grappling with the subtleties and intricacies of doing right by the "others" in our culture, particularly in complex, ambiguous situations.

Beyond that, the Torah asserts that we have an obligation to care not only for other people, but also for the land, as well. This begins with God's command to Adam and Eve with respect to the Garden of Eden, "to till it and tend it" (Gen. 2:15), and it continues with the Torah's demand that, even in war, fruit trees must be preserved (Deut. 20:19–20). The Rabbis expanded on this idea, creating rules dealing with air and water pollution (e.g., Mishnah, *Bava Batra* 2:9; Talmud, *Yevamot* 44a), and ultimately saying, using God's voice, "Pay attention so that you do not spoil or destroy My world, for if you spoil it, there is none to fix it after you" (*Ecclesiastes Rabbah* 7:19). Case 3 raises some contemporary applications of this mandate, which is all the more urgent and complex in our day.

Identifying the mechanisms to sustain human life in a world of more than six billion people, many of whom are polluting our air, water, and food on a daily basis, is a task whose breadth would boggle our ancestors' minds. The essays on Case 3 offer a few different perspectives on how to confront this task on individual, corporate, and civic levels.

Finally, from the time that Cain killed Abel, human beings have done bad things—sometimes with violence. As a result, every society in history has had to deal with criminal justice. The United States currently imprisons a higher percentage of its citizens than any other nation, and federal courts have begun to intervene to force states either to improve their prison facilities or to deal with offenders outside of prisons. Case 4 explores a number of possibilities for meeting these challenges—including alternative sentencing, restorative justice, and victim compensation—that classical American treatments of offenders have ignored. The Jewish tradition has laid out a robust system of justice, and it demands that this system be administered fairly. While it is optimistic that people can change for the better, it also insists that criminals take concrete steps toward rehabilitation before they can again become full members of society. Jewish law also provided for the application of the death penalty, even though it gradually circumscribed the conditions under which that punishment could be used. The responses to Case 4 not only explore the rationales for punishment in contemporary society, but also tackle the controversy regarding the death penalty, a controversy that echoes the ambivalence of Jewish tradition toward that practice.

For each individual and community, determining how to respond to the seemingly endless demands of social justice can be overwhelming. Addressing humanitarian and environmental concerns requires much of us, as does battling discrimination and advocating for a fairer criminal justice system. The wide range of duties that the Jewish tradition imposes on us can make fighting for social justice seem utterly impossible. But we must understand that while we are not meant to carry the world on our shoulders, we must each find a way to fulfill our duty to help repair it. As such, we end this volume with the sage advice of Rabbi Tarfon, who offered a recipe for sanity and responsibility generations ago:

> "You are not required to complete the task, but neither are you free to desist from it." (Mishnah, *Avot* [Ethics of the Fathers] 2:21)

Suggestions for Further Reading

On Social Justice

Alpert, Rebecca. *Voices of the Religious Left*. Philadelphia: Temple University Press, 2008.

Artson, Bradley Shavit and Deborah Silver. *Walking With Justice*. Los Angeles: Ziegler School of Rabbinic Studies, 2008. See www.walkingwith.org.

Brettschneider, Marla, ed. *The Narrow Bridge: Jewish Views on Multiculturalism*. New Brunswick, NJ: Rutgers University Press, 1996.

Dorff, Elliot N. *To Do the Right and the Good: A Jewish Approach to Modern Social Ethics*. Philadelphia: The Jewish Publication Society, 2002.

————. *The Way Into Tikkun Olam (Repairing the World)*. Woodstock, VT: Jewish Lights, 2005.

Jacobs, Jill. *There Shall Be No Needy: Pursuing Social Justice Through Jewish Law and Tradition*. Woodstock, VT: Jewish Lights, 2009.

Rose, Or, Jo Ellen Kaiser, Margie Klein, eds. *Righteous Indignation: A Jewish Call for Justice*. Woodstock, VT: Jewish Lights, 2007.

Sacks, Jonathan. *To Heal a Fractured World: The Ethics of Responsibility*. New York: Schocken, 2007.

Schwarz, Sidney. *Judaism and Justice: The Jewish Passion to Repair the World*. Woodstock, VT: Jewish Lights, 2006.

Tamari, Meir. *"With All Your Possessions": Jewish Ethics and Economic Life*. New York: The Free Press, 1987.

Telushkin, Rabbi Joseph. *A Code of Jewish Ethics, Vol. 2: Love Your Neighbor as Yourself*. New York: Bell Tower, 2009.

Vorspan, Albert and David Saperstein, *Jewish Dimensions of Social Justice: Tough Moral Choices of Our Time*. New York: UAHC Press, 1998.

Walzer, Michael. *Spheres of Justice: A Defense of Pluralism and Equality*. New York: Basic Books, 1983, especially chapters 3, 5, 8, 11, and 13.

Weiss, Avraham. *Spiritual Activism: A Jewish Guide to Leadership and Repairing the World*. Woodstock, VT: Jewish Lights, 2008.

Health Care

Dorff, Elliot N. *Matters of Life and Death: A Jewish Approach to Modern Medical Ethics*. Philadelphia: The Jewish Publication Society, 1998, especially chapter 12, on the distribution and cost of health care.

Steinberg, Avraham. *Encyclopedia of Jewish Medical Ethics*, 3 vols. New York: Feldheim Publishers, 2003, especially volume 1, pp. 40–50.

Zoloth, Laurie. *Health Care and the Ethics of Encounter: A Jewish Discussion of Social Justice*. Chapel Hill, NC: University of North Carolina Press, 1999.

Discrimination and Preferential Treatment

Biale, David, Michael Galchinsky, and Susannah Heschel, eds. *Insider/ Outsider: American Jews and Multiculturalism*. Berkeley, CA: University of California Press, 1998.

Borowitz, Eugene. *Renewing the Covenant: A Theology for the Postmodern Jew*. Philadelphia: The Jewish Publication Society, 1990, especially chapters 12–16.

Dzumra, Noach, ed. *Balancing on the Mechitza: Transgender in Jewish Community*. Berkeley, CA: North Atlantic Books, 2010.

Goldstein, Elyse. *New Jewish Feminism: Probing the Past, Forging the Future*. Woodstock, VT: Jewish Lights, 2008.

Goldstein, Eric. *The Price of Whiteness: Jews, Race, and American Identity*. Princeton, NJ: Princeton University Press, 2007.

Kaplan, Mordecai M. *The Future of the American Jew*. New York: Reconstructionist Press, 1948, especially chapters 8, 13, and 15.

Kaye/Kantrowitz, Melanie. *The Colors of Jews: Racial Politics and Radical Diasporism*. Bloomington, IN: Indiana University Press, 1997.

Ruttenberg, Danya. *Yentl's Revenge: The Next Wave of Jewish Feminism*. Seattle: Seal Press, 2001, especially "Bubbe Got Back: Tales of a Jewess with Caboose" by Ophira Edut and "United Jewish Feminist Front" by Loolwa Khazzoom.

Schneer, David and Caryn Aviv. *Queer Jews*. New York: Routledge, 2002.

The Environment

Benstein, Jeremy. *The Way Into Judaism and the Environment.* Woodstock, VT: Jewish Lights, 2006.

Bernstein, Ellen. *Ecology & the Jewish Spirit: Where Nature and the Sacred Meet.* Woodstock, VT: Jewish Lights, 2000.

"Expanding the Universe of Obligation: Judaism, Justice and Global Responsibility." American Jewish World Service. Available at http://ajws.org/what_we_do/education/resources/core_curriculum/

Tirosh-Samuelson, Hava, ed. *Judaism and Ecology: Created World and Revealed Word.* Cambridge, MA: Center for the Study of World Religions, Harvard Divinity School, 2002.

Waskow, Arthur, ed. *Torah of the Earth: Exploring 4,000 Years of Ecology in Jewish Thought*, 2 vols. Woodstock, VT: Jewish Lights, 2000.

Yaffe, Martin. *Judaism and Environmental Ethics: A Reader.* New York: Lexington Books, 2001.

Crime and Punishment

Cytron, Barry D. and Earl Schwartz. *When Life is in the Balance: Life and Death Decisions in Light of the Jewish Tradition.* New York: United Synagogue of Conservative Judaism Department of Youth Activities, 1986.

Elon, Menachem, Bernard Auerbach, Daniel D. Chazin, and Melvin J. Sykes, eds. *Jewish Law (Mishpat Ivri): Cases and Materials.* New York: Matthew Bender & Co., 1999, especially chapter 15, "Criminal Law."

Gordis, David M., ed. *Crime, Punishment, and Deterrence: A Jewish-American Exploration.* Los Angeles: The Wilstein Institute of Jewish Policy Studies of the University of Judaism, 1991.

Horowitz, George. *The Spirit of Jewish Law.* New York: Central Book Company, 1973, especially chapters 13–15.

Jacob, Walter and Moshe Zemer, eds. *Crime and Punishment in Jewish Law: Essays and Responsa.* New York: Berghahn Books, 1999.

Editors and Contributors

Editors

Elliot N. Dorff, rabbi (Jewish Theological Seminary), Ph.D. (Columbia University), is rector and Sol and Anne Dorff Distinguished Professor of Philosophy at the American Jewish University (formerly the University of Judaism) in Los Angeles. Among the 12 books he has written are four award-winning books on Jewish ethics and law published by The Jewish Publication Society: *Matters of Life and Death* (1998) on Jewish medical ethics; *To Do the Right and the Good* (2002) on Jewish social ethics; *Love Your Neighbor and Yourself* on Jewish personal ethics; and *For the Love of God and People: A Philosophy of Jewish Law* (2007). He has also edited 10 books, including *Contemporary Jewish Ethics and Morality* (Oxford, 1995) and *Contemporary Jewish Theology* (Oxford, 1999), co-edited by Louis Newman, who also co-edited with Dorff the first three volumes of the *Jewish Choices, Jewish Voices* series. Since 1984, Rabbi Dorff has served on the Rabbinical Assembly's Committee on Jewish Law and Standards, and has served as its chair since 2007. He has also served on several federal advisory commissions dealing with the ethics of health care, sexual responsibility, and research on human subjects. He is a member of the State of California's Ethics Committee on embryonic stem cell research. He is married to Marlynn, and they have four children and seven grandchildren.

Danya Ruttenberg, rabbi (Ziegler School of Rabbinic Studies, American Jewish University), is the author of *Surprised By God: How I Learned to Stop Worrying and Love Religion* (Beacon Press, 2008), and editor of *The Passionate Torah: Sex and Judaism* (NYU Press, 2009) and *Yentl's Revenge: The Next Wave of Jewish Feminism* (Seal Press, 2001). She is also a contributing editor to *Lilith* and to the academic journal *Women and Judaism*, serves on the editorial board of *Sh'ma: A Journal of Jewish Responsibility* and Jewschool.com, and has been published in many books and periodicals over the years. Rabbi Ruttenberg, who lives in the Boston area with her husband and son, serves as the Senior Jewish Educator at Tufts University Hillel and teaches and lectures nationwide.

Contributors

Mark Ankcorn, rabbi (Ziegler School of Rabbinic Studies, American Jewish University), J.D. (University of the Pacific, McGeorge School of Law), is a former prosecutor and criminal defense attorney. He served communities as a congregational rabbi in New York City and Florida until 2008, when he returned to Southern California to open his own law firm. Rabbi Ankcorn's law practice concentrates on consumer protection litigation, bankruptcy and complex financial fraud cases, and serious felony appeals. He is an active member of the Beit Midrash Minyan at Congregation Beth Am in San Diego.

Steven Edelman-Blank, rabbi (Ziegler School of Rabbinic Studies of the American Jewish University), is the rabbi of Tifereth Israel Congregation in Des Moines, Iowa. A graduate of Harvard College, he also edited the Contemporary Sources of the first three volumes of this *Jewish Choices/Jewish Voices* series.

Lillian Gelberg, M.D. (Harvard University), M.S.P.H. (UCLA School of Public Health), is George F. Kneller Professor of Family Medicine at the David Geffen School of Medicine at UCLA. She is a health services researcher and family physician who conducts community-based research on the health of homeless and other vulnerable populations, and their access to and quality of care. She is an elected member of the Institute of Medicine of the National Academy of Sciences.

Joseph Gindi is a doctoral student in Religion and Culture at the University of North Carolina at Chapel Hill, where he studies the religious articulation of American Jewish politics. He has an M.A. in Near Eastern and Judaic Studies from Brandeis University and a B.A. in anthropology from Wesleyan University. He is a former residential coordinator of Moishe House Boston: The Kavod Jewish Social Justice House and a former Adamah Fellow.

Justin Goldstein will be ordained as a rabbi by the Ziegler School of Rabbinic Studies of the American Jewish University in 2011. He received his undergraduate degree in Ancient Near Eastern History, Literature, and Language at Hampshire College where he was active in the anti-globalization movement and in organized Jewish life on campus. Since beginning his studies at the Ziegler School, Justin has dedicated much of his time to volunteering and working with organizations such as Progressive Jewish Alliance, Jewish World Watch, Hazon, and Jewish Funds for Justice.

Jo Hirschmann, rabbi (Hebrew Union College), is a chaplain resident at Westchester Medical Center in Valhalla, NY. She has served synagogue communities in Vermont and Pennsylvania and worked as a chaplain at various New York City hospitals. Prior to attending rabbinical school, Jo spent 10 years working in the nonprofit world, including organizations that work on reforming the criminal justice system.

Jill Jacobs, rabbi (The Jewish Theological Seminary), is the author of *There Shall Be No Needy: Pursuing Social Justice through Jewish Law and*

Tradition (Jewish Lights, 2009) and the rabbi-in-residence of Jewish Funds for Justice. A leading expert on Judaism and social justice, she writes and speaks frequently on issues such as poverty, labor relations, housing issues, criminal justice, and environmental sustainability. Rabbi Jacobs was named to *The Forward's* annual list of 50 influential American Jews in 2006 and 2008, to *The Jewish Week's* "36 Under 36" in 2008, and to *Newsweek's* list of the 50 most influential rabbis in 2009. She received an M.A. in Talmud from The Jewish Theological Seminary; an M.S. in Urban Affairs from Hunter College, City University of New York; and a B.A. in Comparative Literature from Columbia University.

Joel Jacobs, J.D. (University of California, Berkeley School of Law), was born and raised in Los Angeles, where he attended Jewish day schools through eighth grade. He graduated from Wesleyan University with a B.A. in Government. He now practices environmental law in the Office of the Attorney General of California in Oakland, although the views expressed in this essay are his alone.

Rachel Kahn-Troster, rabbi (The Jewish Theological Seminary), is director of Education and Outreach for Rabbis for Human Rights-North America. She holds a B.A. from Barnard College and an M.A. in Midrash from The Jewish Theological Seminary. She is a member of the board of Hazon, and a 2009–2010 *D'var Tzedek* writing fellow for the American Jewish World Service. A committed activist and teacher of Jews of all ages, her writing has appeared in *Sh'ma, Conservative Judaism*, and the blogs *The Jew and the Carrot* and Jvoices.com.

Frederick M. Lawrence, J.D. (Yale Law School), is the dean and Robert Kramer Research Professor of Law at The George Washington University Law School. One of the nation's leading civil rights experts, he is the author of *Punishing Hate: Bias Crimes Under American Law* (Harvard University Press, 2002). He has lectured nationally and internationally about bias crime law and has testified before Congress in support of federal hate crimes legislation.

Laurie Levenson, J.D. (University of California, Los Angeles School of Law), is a Professor of Law and David W. Burcham Chair in Ethical Advocacy at Loyola Law School. She teaches criminal law, criminal procedure, ethics, trial advocacy, and evidence. Professor Levenson has authored numerous books and articles, including *Criminal Procedure* (Aspen, 2009), *California Criminal Law* (Thomson-West, 2009), and *The Federal Criminal Rules of Procedure Handbook* (Thomson-West, 2009). She served for eight years as a federal prosecutor in Los Angeles. Professor Levenson received her A.B. from Stanford University, and while she was in law school, she was Chief Articles Editor of the *UCLA Law Review*. She clerked for the Honorable James Hunter III of the U.S. Court of Appeals for the Third Circuit.

Julia Oestreich is a doctoral candidate in History at Temple University and the assistant editor at The Jewish Publication Society. After receiving her B.A. in Government from Smith College, she worked for both the Connecticut and Western Massachusetts branches of the *Jewish Ledger*. She then received her master's degree in Jewish Communal Service from Gratz College. Oestreich has also worked as a curatorial intern for the National Museum of American Jewish History, an instructor for the Florence Melton Mini-Adult School, and a teaching assistant in the Department of History at Temple University. She is project manager of the *Jewish Choices, Jewish Voices* series.

Arthur Waskow, rabbi (ALEPH: Alliance for Jewish Renewal), Ph.D. (University of Wisconsin), directs The Shalom Center (http://www.shalomctr.org), which he founded in 1983. He was a pioneer in developing eco-Judaism, is the author of *Seasons of Our Joy* (Bantam, 1982) and *Down-to-Earth Judaism* (William Morrow, 1995), and is the editor of *Torah of the Earth* (Jewish Lights, 2000) and *Trees, Earth, and Torah* (JPS, 1999). He has initiated numerous Jewishly rooted activist projects through The Shalom Center and its Green Menorah Covenant.

Uzi Weingarten, rabbi (Rabbi Isaac Elchanan Theological Seminary, Yeshiva University), leads seminars in effective, heart-centered communication. He earned a master's degree in Jewish Education from Yeshiva University, and teaches Torah with an emphasis on the message of the Prophets and modern-day psychological insights, focusing on what we can learn to improve our human interactions and spiritual awareness. His website is www.cwcseminars.com.

Shmuly Yanklowitz is a third-year rabbinical student at Yeshivat Chovevei Torah Rabbinical School. He completed his M.A. at Harvard in Moral Psychology and an M.A. at Yeshiva University in Jewish Philosophy. He is now working on his Ph.D. at Columbia University in Epistemology and Moral Development and is an instructor of moral philosophy at Barnard College. He is also a Wexner Graduate Fellow and co-founder and co-director of Uri L'Tzedek (the Orthodox Social Justice Organization).

Index

A

activism, 15–16, 53–54
adoption, 58
adultery, 110
advocacy, 9, 24, 32, 49–50, 53, 83
affirmative action, 36, 44–46, 51–52
African-Americans
    and affirmative action, 36, 51–52
    and capital punishment, 115–16
    and drug-related crimes, 113, 118
    hate crimes against, 65, 67
    incarceration rates, 117–21
    and Jews, 50–52
    racial profiling, 137n21
    and racism in criminal justice system,
        113–14, 115–16, 117–21, 137–38,
        137n21
    understanding of, lack of, 10
air pollution, 80, 89, 97, 98, 141–42
alternative energy, 86, 95
American Jewish Committee (AJC),
    44–45, 49–50
American Jewish Congress (AJCongress),
    49–50, 53
Amir, Yigal, 127
animal waste, 90, 93, 93n10
Anti-Defamation League (ADL), 44,
    49–50, 53
anti-Semitism, 49–51, 54

B

bias crimes. *see* hate crimes
Blackmun, Harry, 136
Black Nationalism, 51–52
Blacks. *see* African-Americans
b'tzelem elohim (in the image of God), 10,
    13, 27, 37, 38, 42, 60–61, 109, 141
Bush, George W., 89n4

C

capital punishment
    and African-Americans, 115–16
    arbitrary nature of, 137
    biblical and rabbinic views on, 106,
        109–12, 123–26
    contemporary Jewish views on, 114–16
    costs of, 138
    as deterrence, 114, 126, 135
    international views on, 105, 139
    in Israel, 115, 127, 140
    manner of execution, 139
    and the poor, 115, 116, 138
    pros and cons, 105–6, 126–28, 134–40
    and witnesses, 110, 115, 135–36
    wrongful conviction/execution,
        115–16, 135–36
CDFI (Community Development
    Financial Institutions), 12
charity *(tzedakah)*. *see also* communal
    funds; justice
    acts of, 5–8
    biblical and rabbinic views of, ix, 5–8,
        16, 20–21
    contemporary Jewish views on, x
    corporate, 26, 31
    and education funding, 119
    and health care, 26, 30–31
    and the environment, 84, 86
    gradations of, 6–7
    Jewish vs. non-Jewish causes, 13
    priorities, 7, 9–10, 21n16
    women receiving, 7
Cheney, Dick, 96
Cities of Refuge, 38, 109–11
citizenship, universal, 47
civic responsibility. *see* governmental
    responsibility
Civil Rights Movement, 47, 50–51

151

Index

Index